THE MEANING OF MUHAMMAD AND OUR CULTURAL MEMORY

SHAYKH FAID MOHAMMED SAID

Published by ISRA Books
Unit 4
5 Durham Yard
London E2 6QF
Israbooks.co.uk

Cover design and Calligraphy: Moustafa Hassan
Graphic design: Mahbub Alam

Printed by Mega Printing in Turkey

Note on the author

Shaykh Faid Mohammed Said is well known for his work in interfaith dialogue and international relations. His keynote speech, "Coexistence in the Modern World", given at a 2012 conference in Istanbul, is here expanded into an entire book.

Shaykh Faid graduated from Madinah University, where he gained his BA Honours in Arabic Language and Islamic Studies with the highest distinction. His world view is shaped by the spirit of Islam, which insists on being "a mercy to all the worlds".

Shaykh Faid encourages Muslims to carry out in their lives the meaning of God's Messenger Muhammad (on him peace and blessings) by preserving his cultural memory and the authentic traditions of Islam.

The same spirit pervades Shaykh Faid's approach in every environment, whether in the world of scholarly activity or in public life. His own life and outlook are important expressions of all that is contained in the blessed tradition. In living in this way Shaykh Faid carries out his own purpose, which is to champion the Messenger and the Message.

Contents

Fig 1: (In Thuluth script), "We sent thee not except as Mercy unto all the worlds." This memorable Qur'an verse encapsulates the meaning of Muhammad – on him peace and blessings

Foreword

An introduction to a written piece of work is customarily understood to mean that which provides basic information about a novel proposal, fresh theory or radically different perspective necessitating explanation of what is to follow. As none of these designations apply to the present work, we think it more fitting to employ the term *foreword*. This at least will spare our respected reader too-high expectations and spare us some discomfort – although any work that aims to shed light on the meaning of Muhammad attains something much more than the dignity of a book. At the same time, a *foreword* allows us some space to guide the reader as he attempts to fit the texts, originally conceived as conference speeches or journal articles in different environments, with the context in which they now appear. In neither their earlier appearance nor in their present form do these writings claim a privileged knowledge about Islam and the Prophet Muhammad (on him peace and blessings). Implicitly, they may be read as a response to certain discouraging assumptions about Islam and, by association, about the Prophet Muhammad. Misrepresentation has gained credence, due in large measure to the unthinking outpourings of a loud few, not to mention the actions of those whose very being was and is the exception that proves the rule. And those assumptions are sustained as much through representation as they are through relative fact.

It is hoped, then, that the reader will receive this work in the spirit of contemplation, while at the same time remaining insightful where the work presents the authentic culture of Islam. The selective interpretation of the Prophetic ideal is neither a defence in the classic sense in that it responds to any particular criticism of the Prophet nor even to the widely apparent negativity directed at Islam as a whole. Wilful or not, misrepresentations of the Prophet and the Divine Message are invariably related to time and place and are not new, as the Qur'an makes clear: *"...It is not thee they reject, but the Divine Messages the offenders deny"* (Q6.33). Since it is ultimately God's Message and delivered by His Messenger, we need not unduly exert ourselves in taking an apologetic tone, even though the Messenger and the Message are inseparable. Lady 'Aisha the wife of the Prophet, responded to questions about the Prophet's character with the emphatic reply, "The Prophet's character was the Qur'an" (Muslim). It is hoped that the representation of the Prophetic true example, which is explicitly the aim of the present work, will re-enlighten both those who identify themselves as Muslims and other readers in a deeper appreciation of the meaning of Muhammad. Indeed, God says, *"We never sent you but as a Messenger unto all mankind, conveying to them glad tidings and forewarning them, but most of them know not"* (Q34.28). And indeed God says *"We sent thee not except as Mercy unto all the worlds"* (Q21.107).

The body of this work provides pointers to the multi-faceted picture of civilisation-in-Islam and Islamic culture, a culture shaped on the example of the Prophet Muhammad. It explores values shared with all humanity, with liberation of thought and of expression. The unmistakeable feature of this culture of Islam was and still is the Prophetic paradigm. This Islamic culture is not a posthumous glorification of a romantic past, nor is it a myth perpetuated by adherents in the present day. But the culture to which we apply the term Prophetic paradigm was readily accepted in Christian Abyssinia, transformed the Mediterranean and Asiatic worlds of Rome and Persia, won admiration in Indo-China and later held Europe captivated. Its spirit was both appealing and liberating. The clear and quantifiable aspect of this culture, its tone and nature, was *mercy* in all its signs and significations. Sympathy and benevolence, grace and understanding, the highest regard for humanity were all at its core. The meaning, although it may not always have been obvious to outsiders, nonetheless drew them to what this culture represented. The insiders who cherished and maintained the paradigm knew the meaning of Muhammad, as a *"Mercy to all the worlds"*. The meaning of Muhammad was for them always the yardstick of being, of social interaction, of what it means to be the best of creation. And let this statement not be taken lightly, for Muhammad is indeed the best of creation and we are only too happy to stress the point. God affirms this by the life of the Prophet, the embodiment of His mercy: *"Indeed, by thy life, O Prophet, in their wild intoxication they wander in distraction"* (Q15.72). Affirming the Prophet's life as the subject of the divine oath, Abdullah ibn 'Abbas, even in his own lifetime recognised as the Qur'an scholar par excellence, declared *"Never does God swear by human life in the Qur'an except the life of the Blessed Prophet, in whom God perfected life"* (Qadi Iyad, and Tabari).

The lack of constancy in Muslims has wrought something much worse than the degeneration of civilisation, which is commonly understood in terms of historic rise and fall. It has meant the cultural decline and loss of memory of the meaning of Muhammad. So long as the culture of the Muslims was instinctively *"Muhammadan"*, it was benevolent, compassionate and liberating. Once full of vitality, the culture now is marked by despair and consequential destructiveness. Much energy is expended in talk about revival. But, in its uncaring long march, history is usually intolerant of revivalism, so it is not a matter of revival but of renewal. And Muslim culture, although now warped and distorted almost beyond recognition in its own mirror, still contains within it the will to effect renewal, not by attempting to revive time-bound past forms but by reaffirming the timeless meaning of Muhammad. Renewal is possible through the reaffirmation of the Prophetic paradigm, by being truly *"Muhammadan"* as a *"mercy unto the worlds"*.

What is in the memory? To what extent can we claim to understand the meaning of Muhammad? Let us recall a story relating to 'Umar ibn al-Khattab and Al Hurru ibn Qais. They were companions of the Prophet. At the time there was a real desire for learning and understanding, this was irrespective of age, social rank or parochial identity. Al Hurru would take shelter in scholarly circles and his regular companion was 'Umar ibn al-Khattab, at the time the second Caliph of Islam. On one occasion Al-

Hurru's uncle had unfairly accused the tirelessly charitable Umar of meanness. Knowing of his uncle's unfairness, Al Hurru calmed down 'Umar with an appeal for restraint. *"O Chief of the Believers, recall God's saying, 'Hold to forgiveness and enjoin what is right but turn away from the ignorant'"* (Q7.199, ibn 'Abbas). Also Imam 'Ja'far as-Sadiq, a grandson of the Prophet, described the verse as the "essence of Islam and contains an abundance of good for humanity". This verse, both in its literal and implied meanings, represents the core of Muslim culture.

Let us also recall an example from 'Abu Bakr as-Siddiq, the first Caliph. He was once understandably reluctant to maintain a charitable disposition towards one of his kinsmen, 'Mistah ibn Athaatha, following the latter's role in spreading slander about his daughter Lady 'Aisha, the Prophet's wife. 'Mistah who had been orphaned at the age of four, was entirely dependent on 'Abu Bakr. A distraught 'Abu Bakr vowed to sever ties with the young man. He was nonetheless influenced by the Qu'ranic verse: *"Let not those among you who have both grace and ample means resolve by oath against helping their kinsmen, those in want and those who have left their homes in God's cause; let them forgive and overlook. Do you not wish that God should forgive you? And God is Ever-Forgiving, Most Merciful"* (Q24.22). Overlooking the difficulty placed on his family as a result of the slandering, 'Abu Bakr matched his forbearance by doubling his expenditure on the chastened 'Mistah's welfare. In personality there is no sharper contrast between the passionate 'Umar and the placid 'Abu Bakr, yet their superior nature was always unquestionably in the Muhammadan paradigm.

The Prophet Muhammad always encouraged the adherence to universal precepts. In the Judaeo-Christian tradition we find that Abraham was always eager to invite even strangers to share his food. On one occasion he offered food to a stranger on condition that he submitted to God. Abraham was promptly admonished by God. *"O Abraham, you have linked your generosity to Me. I am free of all need yet I provide sustenance to all. But you would not share my kindness with a portion of food."* Abraham is considered the father of prophets and is revered by all three faiths of Judaism, Christianity and Islam. In this story Abraham learnt the meaning of unconditional generosity, which is beyond colour, caste or creed. God says in the Qur'an, *"Say ye; 'We believe in God and the revelation given to us, to Abraham, Ismail, Isaac, Jacob and the tribes. To Moses, Jesus and all Prophets. We make no difference between one another of them and we are of those who submit to God"* (Q2.136). From this verse we learn that God continued His covenant with those who had gone before and the Muslims were to affirm their covenant with God by accepting that there is "no god but God and Muhammad is His Messenger". In so doing, Muslims would abandon all idols including the one that resides within them. In so doing, they accept all prophets past and become truly Muhammadan in the state of their submission.

Muslims are asked to *"...consider with kindness parents and kindred, orphans and those in need; announce yourself magnanimously to the people..."* (Q2.83). Muslims are sworn to embrace the culture of kindness and magnanimity, of spreading good forms of behaviour. This is the meaning of being Muhammadan. To extend kindness is the very substance of the universal moral compass and to speak fairly and benevolently is its indicator. We must remember that Muslims of today are not removed from the moral compass associated with the meaning of Muhammad.

If we speak about a Muslim culture without the Muhammadan aspect the culture is quite disorientated and confusing. It may be argued that the conditions for an authentic Muslim culture can be ensured by the type of socio-political system in place. But such an argument can be turned on its head as one might say, Muslim culture, if faithful to itself and therefore Muhammadan in its aspect, can transform or co-exist in any system (to co-exist is to transform by mutual exchange). Certainly the culture of the

Muslims that we speak of was sustained and even flourished in a variety of often problematic systems and localities. In addition, once the era of the historic and rightly-guided Caliphate was over, the cultural and the political lives of Muslims were often remarkably independent of each other, to the extent that the culture was able to continue alongside immoral rule or corrupt systems. In this connection, the outstanding fourth Caliph 'Ali Ibn abi Talib and his exemplary sons, Imam Hassan and Imam Hussain, will be forever remembered. Imam Hassan ibn 'Ali Ibn abi Talib embodied the Muslim culture that bore all of the Muhammadan features and not simply because he was the grandson of the Prophet. As already pointed out, culture and politics can be unrelated to each other and this was especially so in the period after the death of the third Caliph, Uthman ibn 'Affan.

While seeing the early Caliphate as an impressive phenomenon in terms of rapid and great territorial enlargement, it is also worth remembering that the pace of expansion and geographical reach meant that the dominion was never a stable entity. Many stalwarts of Muslim culture were caustically critical of developments and feared the culture's sudden exposure to power, wealth and influence, or at least to the inevitable scramble for them, would result in a loss of identity.

Following the martyrdom of Imam 'Ali ibn abi Talib, his eldest son Imam Hassan, despite enjoying majority support, declined to stake his claim to the Caliphate through force (As-Suyuti). Imam Hassan was in every aspect his father's son, gallant, saintly and universally respected. He characteristically abdicated leadership to spare the Muslims further discord when rival claimants emerged. It was not the corrosive effects of power that Imam Hassan feared, rather the adverse conditions of his time. This further illuminates his chivalry and his deep concern for his fellow men. The culture that insists on its Muhammadan aspect thus bears testimony that Muslims can affirm their authentic identity in any environment. In many respects the Muhammadan culture is still the dominant identity of the

Muslims, albeit embarrassed and silent in the shadows, with its memory clouded. Imam Hassan's conscience was governed by his grandfather's culture, in that instance the spirit of cheerful self-sacrifice for the sake of a greater good. Embracing his grandson in his arms, the Prophet had said of the child Hassan, *"Know ye all that this son of mine be a master. Through him shall God unite two large groups of the people"* (Bukhari). As a peace-maker and unifying force and as one bearing the appellation *"Imam"*, this is indeed suitable. In fact, the cultural legacy handed down by Imam Hassan is immeasurable; having withdrawn to a life of quiet contemplation in Madinah, his scholarly pursuit in voluntary retirement has proved a benefit for his cultural inheritors.

When we speak of cultural memory, cultural inheritance, and the Muhammadan Muslim culture it is impossible to do so without giving mention to Imam Ali ibn abi Talib. In his Syrian campaign the Caliph had broken off the bloody engagement at the battle of Siffin because of the sudden wavering of his Kharijite allied faction. Victory at Siffin had looked imminent for Imam 'Ali, before the battlefield fiasco in which copies of the Quran were placed on the spearheads by the army of 'Muawiyah. A farcical arbitration followed, urged on loudest by the Kharijites when they abandoned Imam 'Ali. Their dubious claims to divine truth undermined the Caliph's spiritual authority and yet Imam 'Ali's response to Kharijite provocation remains as peerless as it is exemplary. Even when the Kharijites turned increasingly hostile, 'Ali counselled vigilance while declining opportunities for pre-emptive strikes against them. In a period of great confusion, to which some of today's sectarian fractures can be traced, the Caliph, seeking reconciliation, refused to cast them as heretics and further declared that he would not disbar them from communal prayer.
Imam 'Ali was well aware of the dangers of a powerful dissenting group; it might have been expedient to strip the Kharijites of the means to make more trouble but he let them retain war-spoils from the campaign. It must

be said the Kharijites, unlike other new converts, were not swayed by the prospect of booty. As the forces of the Caliphate carved open Byzantine Syria and Persian Iraq (Baihaqi, ibn abi Shaybah), the Kharijites soon turned disloyal. Modern thought may well regard the Caliph's actions as quaintly idealistic but none can deny what is exemplary. Imam 'Ali's devoted benevolence, justice, magnanimity and integrity in the face of insubordination is plain for all to see. But then Imam Ali had been exposed to the mercy of the Prophet from his birth since he had been brought up in the house where the Prophet lived. He was clement and generous to all groups and factions. Imam 'Ali could only act thus because his character and culture sought to preserve the Muhammadan paradigm.

Imam 'Ali's younger son, Imam Hussain, had to contend with numerous injustices as his father had done before him. He had fought in his father's campaigns, stood tall with his brother and was united with them in martyrdom when he and very nearly all the male members of his family were mercilessly killed at Karbala (in modern day Iraq). The reaction of his son Imam Ali Zain al-Abedin, the sole male survivor of the Karbala massacre, sums up the magnanimity of those who were heirs to the Prophet's spiritual and temporal legacy. Like his forefathers, he never sought vengeance for the grievous injuries inflicted on the family. They had striven to safeguard the Muslim commonwealth, offering up their own lives in the process, so he too exerted himself for the commonwealth with life and limb, quite literally.

On his death, tradition says Imam Ali Zain al-Abedin's upper limbs were found to be blackened as a result of years of carrying and secretly distributing foodstuffs and other provisions to the destitute in Madinah. His selflessness and benefaction had posthumously come to light when poor residents of Madinah were concerned as to why their provisions had abruptly ended (Siyaar A'lam An-Nubaala). The great scholar and historian Muhammad ibn Ishaq said there were very many people in Madinah who received provisions at night and who puzzled over the source of their supplies, realising the identity of their benefactor only after the death of Imam Ali Zain al-Abedin. Ibn Ishaq also mentioned the Imam's scorched limbs and recounts that as many as 100 families had benefited from his secret sponsorship (Adh-Dhahabi). Indeed, the leading Madani scholar of the day, Az-Zuhri, swore that he had *"never known one more knowledgeable than Imam Ali Zain al-Abedin the son of Hussain' (Ad-Dhahabi), while others esteemed their own prized pedagogic chains going back to the greatest teacher of all... ...it is Az-Zuhri from Ali Zain al Abedin from Hussain ibn Ali from Ali ibn abi Taalib"* (Ibn abi Shaybah). The environment created by the exemplars of this culture was such that, although verities were often distorted, the justice and chivalry that marked their life-experiences illustrate some of what is best about Muslim culture, timelessly Muhammadan if it is lived, but mere footnotes in books if the memory is lost.

And so the sole purpose of this work is to remind all those of us who identify ourselves as Muslims by testifying that "there is no god but God" and *"Muhammad is His Messenger"*, that belief in the full statement brings with it the responsibility to emulate God's Messenger Muhammad to be a mercy unto all the worlds. It is within us, for it is our cultural inheritance. By refreshing our memories we reaffirm ourselves as being Muhammadan. Only then are we ready to be *"a mercy unto all the worlds"*. Our Prophet Muhammad is the one who sealed our culture with his identity, fashioned it in his likeness, and said "Be conscious of God wherever you are and when you go astray be prepared to erase error through what is virtuous. And show to all mankind the best of character" (Tirmidhi). The scholar Imam Nawa'wi specially included this in his celebrated *"Forty Hadith"*, because of three underlying principles contained within it. God-consciousness, a stress on optimism over despair and a humane outlook filled with compassion. Muslims can no longer limit their vision and practice to their own historical landscapes, not when we recast our memories and realise that we are meant to be a mercy unto the worlds. We do not attempt to retrieve the past, for the past is always present as we are still Muhammadan. We cannot avoid the present as we look towards the future, to be nearest to the best of Creation. The holy Prophet said *"Nearest to me are those with the best of character"* (Tirmidhi). The Messenger who was sent as a Mercy unto all the worlds also said, *"Extend mercy to all God's Creation, then the Most Merciful shall cover you with His Mercy"* (Tirmidhi).

Faid Mohammed Said

Fig 2: (In Thuluth script), "In the Name of Allah, the Most Gracious, the Dispenser of Grace" and "It is not thee they reject, but the Divine Messages the offenders deny." Although the Messenger and the Message are inseparable, misrepresentations and misinterpretations abound

Between reality and representation

The present work arose out of ideas first discussed at an international symposium at the end of 2012 in Istanbul, Turkey. Participants shared thoughts about *"Islam and coexistence"*. Our own effort focused on the personality of the Prophet Muhammad and the example he set Muslims in becoming a beacon to humanity. In relation to the anxiety-driven questions about peaceful coexistence in our contemporary world, we also discussed, briefly, the gap between reality and representation where it concerned Islam and Muslims. Now as then, time and space preclude a full-length examination of the Prophet's ultimate legacy. A theory and practice of peaceful coexistence marked by the Prophet's own ministry and mission was a salient feature of Muslim societies at their most enlightened. The present discussion aims to fill a small part of that gap, while situating this work alongside current debates about culture and social cohesion.

Among the many scholarly works and popular discourses debated and written about human relations in the contemporary world, the overwhelming majority have done so from the vantage point of the Euro-American worldview, almost always crudely generalised in terms of *the West and the rest*. Globalisation and technological levelling have done much to dissolve this binary opposition, yet there still persists notions of the *other*, almost always Islam and its adherents, once located and contained in the East but now perceived as a clear and present danger to the societies of the West.

Such assertions risk becoming a gross simplification, not least because the dominant culture of the Western worldview faces internal and external resistance from disparate cultural groupings. However, we mean it here in a broad sense in order to specify a complex of anxieties about Islam and Muslims which operates in a tangle of reality and fiction. Perceptions about Muslims may well have been determined by centuries of religious difference, but are also exacerbated by popular representations of this group as intolerant and unable to integrate.

Thus, it seems positively necessary to collapse all who claim to be Muslim into a unified entity and see them as an obstacle to the progress of the human race in general and a danger to Western civilization in particular. For, co-existent with the notion of a progressive Western civilization is the idea of Muslims and Islam as an irrational, intolerant and backward aspect of modern humanity. It is hardly necessary to examine stereotyped images of Muslims and their demonisation in our time and yet it must be acknowledged that particular circumstances and phenomena have been instrumental in both creating and sustaining such perceptions about Muslims. Indiscriminate violence and intolerance have intensified fears of being menaced by this incomprehensible *other*.

Contemporary mass media representations of Islam and Muslim cultural traditions have followed the tendency to portray both Muslims and Islamic civilization as outside of history and hopelessly in need of reform. Cultural discourses mimic the popular representation of Muslims as reactionary, misogynistic and unable or unwilling to assimilate. Still, a view that argues this way not only overlooks the contribution of Muslims, denying them any agency, but in so doing acquires the very characteristics of intolerance that it has assigned to the *other*. Certainly within some Muslim cultures there is much that deserves just such an interpretation but an open approach would reveal much more that is positive about Islam and the authentic culture of Islam.

Our approach here is informed by the archaeological methods that prevail in cultural studies and are applied to the examination of social interaction in settings where Muslims and non-Muslims have both constituted parts of those societies. Such a disciplinary method is particularly useful when elements of a text, be it revealed Scripture, recorded oral tradition or literary production, are grounded within a socio-historical context. By paying attention to the social contexts within which texts originate and flourish, combined with careful attention to the texts themselves, what emerges is a genuine theory and practice of peaceful coexistence in Islam's history generally and one that bears the imprint of the Prophet in particular. Above all, such practices played an important role, not only in the way individuals formed their own ideas, but they also influenced the formation of their societies.

With these considerations in mind, a prime focus of the present discussion is the extent to which Islam from the very beginning established a way of life that insisted on tolerance, generosity and harmonious coexistence. One is struck by the Prophet's unerring knack of being able to bridge cultural divides, fuse diverse elements, abandon identity politics in favour of social harmony and find common cause while yet being able to celebrate difference. The Prophet's example represents the highest degree of tolerance, kindness and justice and he was the single most important shaping influence on his contemporaries, one that influenced all or most aspects of their lives.

In the first part of the present work a striking selection of instances reveals the Prophet's approach to sometimes unresponsive and hostile neighbours in the public sphere, as well as providing deeply illuminating personal stories relating to his private life. The interplay between the existing social system in Madinah and the Prophet's responses to it as it played out in the culture of the time is examined in the second part, with special focus on the function of the Madinah Declaration. This document, arguably the world's first-ever charter of enshrined rights and liberties, was instrumental in the formation of an inclusive civic religion. Enjoining mutual dependence and social harmony, not only in the lifetime of its initiator, the Prophet Muhammad, the plurality and multiculturalism it embraced is inherent in the authentic culture of Islam. The retrieval of a short story from tenth century Muslim Spain in the third part illuminates this faithful inheritance and expression of the Muhammadan culture in one of Islamic civilization's greatest centres. The final part gestures at the contemporary debates within which this work is placed while connecting them with the thematic preoccupations of the sections that follow.

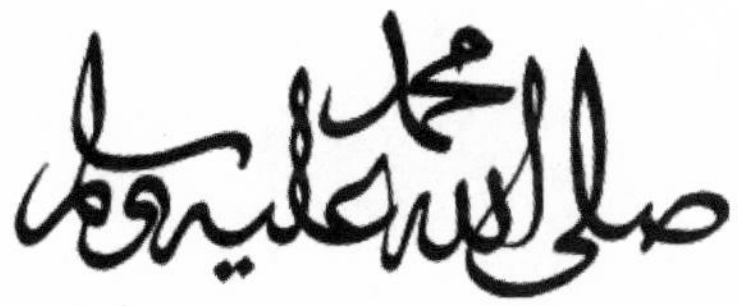
محمد
صلى الله عليه وسلم

Fig 3 "Peace and Blessings upon him" – the customary invocation upon the Prophet Muhammad

The Prophetic Paradigm

In Makkah the Prophet Muhammad had to contend with those who not only rejected his worldview but for many years subjected him and his companions to severe hostility and persecution. Before the mass migration to Madinah the Muslim community in Makkah suffered physical and verbal abuse, social and economic exclusion and forced displacement. Enjoying overwhelming might and power, the Makkans exulted in their flagrant aggression. However, in Madinah the Muslims faced different kinds of opposition in an environment where they enjoyed some semblance of security.

In and around Madinah the interests of three groups, the native Arabs who claimed allegiance to Islam, the native Jews and the still-pagan Arabs, converged so that they had to contend with foes pretending friendship. Resenting loss of former influence, some native Arabs outwardly professed Islam but on various levels frequently undermined the Prophet. One might have expected condemnation of this two-faced grouping in the Qur'an as justification for punitive measures against them. But the response of the Prophet was to patiently invite them into Islam. Instead of adopting a too-easy interpretation of divine censure to punish them, he was extraordinarily lenient with the subversive elements in his society. Limiting himself to general warnings about hypocrisy, he never exposed their identity out of concern that his own loyal companions might exact retribution. Only 'Hudhayfah ibn al-Yaman, his secretary, was privy to his dismay.

The Prophet's attitude is breath-taking, a sizeable element was brazenly conniving with enemies and yet he consciously chose not to expose them. We may be tempted to think it a dangerous policy, this clement treatment of the subversive group led by one Abdullah ibn Ubay. Put into context, the Muslim community faced considerable danger and ibn Ubay's treachery included battlefield desertion and unabashed collusion with the Prophet's enemies. However, the striking feature of such clemency was that ibn Ubay's party, the much-maligned hypocrites, were eventually won over, even as the son of ibn Ubay remained a staunch Muslim all along.

Informed on arrival in Madinah that the native Jews annually fasted on the tenth day of the month of Muharram in thanksgiving for Moses' victory over Pharaoh, the Holy Prophet exhorted the Muslims to also observe a fast on that day, declaring, *"I am closer to Moses than they."*[1] He taught the Muslims that Moses' victory was their victory because all prophets strive for the same goal, while demonstrating to the Jewish constituency that he shared their values and found their custom appealing. As far as the Prophet was concerned, the personal always was the political. One of his wives, the Lady 'Safia bint Huyay, famously traced descent from the line of Aaron and of Moses. Although she had happily embraced Islam, the Lady 'Safia was derided by her fellow wives for her Jewishness until the Prophet taught her the unanswerable challenge, *"My father was a prophet, my uncle was a prophet and I am the wife of a prophet."*[2] Disavowing discrimination in any form, this sketch of life within the Prophetic household simultaneously shows how the Prophet was always readily able to transcend barriers of race and religion even as he encouraged his wife to be proud of her own ethnic identity.

The exaggerated difference between Jew and Muslim in our time would have appalled both the early Muslims and the Jewish communities with whom they lived cheek-by-jowl. Standing up from a reclining position to mark respect for a Jewish funeral procession, the Prophet was questioned about this and simply replied, *"Is it not a human soul?"*[3] Troubled by the absence of a Jewish boy in his service, the Prophet was informed that the youth was fatally sick and went to visit him. Invited to recognise him as God's Messenger, the dying youth looked to his father. The latter, resolute in his faith, nonetheless recognised the Prophet's benevolent concern and urged his son to "follow Abul-Qasim."[4] There was no obvious gain in the material world for either party from the conversion of one about to expire, so the only motivation was the sincere concern of the one and the willing acceptance by the other. It was common humanity that induced the Prophet's visit. Jews and pre-Islamic Arabs in Madinah had in any case enjoyed cross-cultural interaction, including inter-marriage. After the Prophet's arrival in Madinah these traditions were enhanced and he set the pattern for community contact and mutual exchange in civil society to the very end of his life. On his death, the Prophet's companions discovered that his shield was mortgaged with a Jew.[5]

The Prophet's clemency and forbearance, given expression in his embrace of plurality and diversity, represents the authentic culture of Islam. So it is that in the life of the Prophet Muhammad we find a timeless model for all humanity. *"Indeed in God's Messenger you have the outstanding example."*[6]

The Meaning of Muhammad and Our Cultural Memory

Fig 4: (In Thuluth script), "In the Name of Allah, the Most Gracious, the Dispenser of Grace" and "We sent thee not but as a Messenger unto all mankind, conveying to them glad tidings and forewarning them, but most of them know not." There is a pressing need to understand the meaning of Muhammad while humanity struggles for justice and peace

Theory and Practice

The rigid social system in Makkah was seriously undermined in the early years of Islam, which facilitated movement across social barriers, emancipating and empowering disadvantaged groups. But it was the Muslim experience in Madinah that witnessed the growth of a truly pluralistic society. The famous Madinah Declaration would forever be associated with the Prophet's city because of the social charter ratified there, conferring individual liberties and civic responsibilities upon the disparate communities who signed up to the document. Intimately linked to this charter of rights and enshrined freedoms in the emergent state of Madinah was the personal history of its originator, the Prophet Muhammad.

Built on a network of tribal alliances, the delicate balance of power in Madinah had shifted decisively with the arrival of the Muslim émigrés from Makkah. The internecine war between Aws and the Khazraj, the two Arab tribes in Madinah, had come to an end following their embrace of Islam, although not all the indigenous Arabs of Madinah had entered the fold. Joined by the Makkans, the Muslims now became the majority community in Madinah, unified through religion.

The Aws and the Khazraj had formerly built alliances with the three dominant Jewish tribes in Madinah but these had overnight become obsolete. The Aws and Khazraj had also enjoyed complex affiliations with outlying desert tribes so that, all in all, power relations were completely transformed and the Prophet found himself leader of the newly-dominant constituency. Far from issuing orders to the minority communities, he embarked on an integration programme that extended well beyond mere pacification. Through the instrument of the Madinah Declaration he conferred equal rights on the various participants in the now-unified state, in the process granting its signatories the distinction of becoming the first-ever human community to enjoy a charter of rights.[7] The status of the immigrants, namely the Makkan refugees, also changed dramatically. Any anxieties about their deracination or reduction to second-class citizens in the new environment were soon dispelled. Article Four of the Declaration ensured that all Madinans had the same right of redress under law. In the first instance it enshrined equality in law so that a native of Madinah had no greater right than an immigrant or naturalized citizen. Second, that law was self-referentially Madinan, meaning that the Makkans wholly embraced the laws of the host nation.

The Declaration made explicit the equality conferred upon all parties. Various articles of the instrument proclaim the *"indiscriminate rule of law and justice for all communities"* and the *"prohibition of unjust favouritism"*, that "non-Muslim minorities possess the same right to life protection" and the *"guarantee of freedom of faith for both Muslims and non-Muslims"*. The Declaration recognised differences among its signatories as evidenced by Article 40 which granted *"equality of rights for all branches of the Jews"*. In this regard, the various divisions that exist within Islam would do well to rethink their relations. Differences might not be so irreconcilable; certainly there is nothing to prevent harmonious co-existence.

While the Madinah Declaration was very much a product of its historic context, the tenets enshrined – freedom of belief, equality in law and recognition - and consequent protection - of differences. These are fundamental principles of Islam and of its culture. Freedom of belief is explicit in the Qur'an, which over and over confirms this principle. It is of paramount importance if peaceful coexistence is to achieve real meaning.

Compulsion in belief is explicitly forbidden: *"There is no compulsion in belief, for truth stands out clear from error."*[8] Thus in the Islamic perspective God has granted His Creation freedom of choice: *"Whosoever wishes, let him believe and whosoever will, let him disbelieve."*[9] Moreover, God confirms that one of the requirements of His cosmic order is diversity: *"Had God willed, He would have made you one community."*[10] Recognition

of the *other* is an equally important logical extension of freedom of belief
and here *"belief"* means, not simply religious alignment, but something
approaching "way of life" or "culture". Hence in the Qur'an: *"Unto you,
your belief and unto me, my belief."*[11] The chapter containing this verse is
revealingly entitled, *"The Unbelievers"*. The verse begins the chapter thus:
"Say, O Unbelievers!"[12] The Qur'an thereby gave to Islam's culture its
particular hue when it established not only freedom of choice but also
recognition of another's belief, ideology and inclination.

When seen in its natural way, the generosity and open-handedness of the
authentic culture of Islam confounds even its staunchest critic. Now-
customary arguments against organised religion include fear of total
enslavement and yet closer inspection reveals that the God of Islam offers
complete freedom of choice. By no means is this a rarefied position. It
was in this manner that the Prophet and his followers long received,
understood and sustained the Qur'an. When Islam is viewed this way it
appears surprising modern and far from the common idea that it stuck in
the Middle Ages. This again confounds totalitarian conceptions about
Islam. At the very least, such an understanding of Islam leads to the
opening-up of more positive dialogue with it. The scholarly community of
Islam frequently says, *"The key to the Qur'an is the Qur'an."* Or we might
say the puzzle contains its own solution. On the other hand the
proclamations of a host of noisy Muslims do not make Islam very
appealing, much less comprehensible. The Qur'an states: *"Do you enjoin
right conduct upon mankind while you neglect (its practice) yourselves?
And you read the Scripture!"*[13]

Unsurprisingly, even the most enlightened efforts at coexistence will
degenerate if the approach and application are faulty. Efforts at
interpersonal and social relations are contingent upon communication at its
finest and according to all that is best in manners, without loquacity or
intimidation. The Qur'an exhorts benevolence in dialogue even in the face

of received offence: "And argue not with the People of the Scripture unless in a way that is better."[14] The stress on gentle persuasion in this Qur'anic verse is more than a call for objective reasoning. Generosity means sincere goodwill and not merely grudging acceptance. The Qur'an's exhortation to adopt only the best speech is especially instructive because mankind is greatly esteemed by God: *"Indeed, We have honoured the children of Adam."*[15] The point is not whether one is a theist, polytheist or an atheist but that the human being occupies a lofty position, reflected in the mode and manner in which we respond to differences of opinion and belief.

The Madinah Declaration was unique to its historic context but freedom of belief, equality in law and recognition of difference are universal principles in Islam. If the commitment to rights and liberties is the goal of modern humans, then these were set in stone by the last of the prophets but first among modernists, and that was Muhammad. Seventh-century forms are long out of fashion but these principles are timeless and this spirit is enlivening in every age.

Fig 5: (In Thuluth script), "In the Name of Allah, the Most Gracious, the Dispenser of Grace" and "Hold to forgiveness, and enjoin what is right; but turn away from the ignorant." This verse is a special feature of the Muhammadan culture

Raise the spirit, rest the form

"See you not how God commands us to show common courtesy? As Minister of State, the honourable Abdun ibn Sa'eed is servant to you, the Muslims, and he is the connection between you, the people, and your Caliph. Moreover, this man has come to us even as we cannot approach others in the land."[16]

Why retrieve an anecdote about a Muslim scholar from the cultural history of Europe in the tenth century, particularly in a discussion about coexistence in our contemporary world? Given that this discussion aims to provoke thought about an authentic Islam and its representational practices in terms of history, culture and society, it is a transparent choice. With a gulf between enlightened principles and practical reality, faith traditions, not least Islam, are overlooked in the search for viable models and solutions to the social and political problems of the twenty-first century. The Qur'an lays great stress on shared harmony where there is no manifest ill-intent or aggression against any one person or community for reasons of religious belief, utterly refuting acts of violence or incitement to violence against the social body. Can we learn anything from the principles espoused by Islam when its adherents enjoyed cultural and socio-economic power? And what might an authentic Islam contribute to questions of social harmony and peaceful coexistence nowadays?

The relationship between peoples of diverse faith traditions during the tenth-century in Muslim Spain is especially significant to a discussion on cultural identity and coexistence in the modern world. Islam in the Iberian peninsula of Europe at this time represented for Muslims and non-Muslims alike a special model for the development of harmonious communal relations, one that offers important lessons to our time. Indeed, the cross-cultural relations prevalent in the original European Muslim experience – marked by heterogeneity and plurality – was more or less equivalent to the multicultural coexistence now claimed to be the special privilege of Euro-American models of plurality and polymorphous societies.

Qadi Abu Ishaq Ismail ibn Ishaq, the foremost Maliki jurist, was a scion of the family of Hamid ibn Zaid, famed for its great learning and nobility for more than 300 years. While in the company of his students and peers, Qadi was once visited by Abdun ibn Sa'eed, a formidably able Minister of State, and a devout Christian. Qadi stood up to receive the Minister and the two men proceeded to discuss matters of state. After Abdun ibn Sa'eed had departed, Qadi's students queried the appropriateness of rising to his feet in deference to a Christian.

Qadi was not the least bit flustered by this. With a serene smile, he responded with a Qur'anic verse: *"God forbids you not to regard those who do not fight you on account of your faith, nor drive you from your homes, from dealing kindly and justly with them; for God loves those who are just."*[17] Delighted by his students' critical independence, Qadi patiently explained his reception of the Minister thus: *"See how God commands us to show common courtesy? As Minister of State, the honourable Abdun ibn Sa'eed is servant to you, the Muslims, and he is the connection between you, the people, and your Caliph. Moreover, this man has come to us even as we cannot approach others in the land."* Born in 200AH (After Hijirah), Qadi Abu Ishaq Ismail ibn Ishaq lived in the third century after the Prophet, his death in 282AH represented almost the end of a chapter of unbounded grace.

One of the great scholars of Islam knew well enough to honour a Christian, but some Muslims now quibble whether to send condolences to a non-Muslim. And yet we have seen how, from the very beginning, Islam established an aesthetic and material reality that insisted and encouraged tolerance, generosity and harmonious coexistence. The Islamic civilization of Andalusia considerably influenced the later Renaissance across much of southern and western Europe.

Narratives that relate the history of Islam in Iberia and in North Africa rightly focus on the vastly enlightening contribution of Muslim scholarship, both in terms of its own originality and its revival and preservation of ancient Greek learning. A constituent of such scholarly brilliance and expansiveness of mind was the manner in which Islam's followers engaged with adherents of other faiths and belief systems. The cultural traditions built by the early scholars of Islam enlightened more than their own co-religionists and made Andalusia a magnet for men and women of learning from all over the world, particularly those who cherished ideas about personal freedom and social harmony. It was not the fire and the sword but the Prophet's legacy of tolerance and respect that made Islam and the Muslims so appealing.

Islamic texts made recommendations appropriate to the time, while responding to and shaping contemporary social conditions. The significance of such texts also related to customary practices in societies populated by Muslims or indeed where Muslims constituted a portion of the populace. Studying the reception and application of those practices enables us to learn about the behaviour, attitudes, manners and morals of those societies.

Looking through a variety of texts, from the Qur'an to Prophetic traditions and later cultural productions within different historical contexts, the reader notes the number of issues that still resonate in our time. These include matters of coexistence, difference, self-image and perceptions of the *other*.

It is important to stress again that there is a need to celebrate those aspects of peaceful coexistence which are most valuable since finding similarity in difference lies at the heart of human relations. One sure way is to rethink and re-examine the life of the Prophet Muhammad. We might say the Prophet's title as *"a mercy unto all the worlds"* aptly sums up all that he taught and demonstrated through his own personal behaviour.

The Meaning of Muhammad and Our Cultural Memory

Fig 6: (In Diwani script), "O people, I am a mercy unto you..." To embrace a culture of kindness and magnanimity is the true meaning of being Muhammadan

Re-turn to the culture of Islam

The discourses organised around coexistence have acquired added urgency in a world driven by technology, which has shrunk space in proportion to the relentless expansion of human interaction and the global mass exchange of information. The great developments brought about by instant communication have also transformed the nature of experience so that it is now impossible for societies to focus exclusively on their own internal affairs or to pursue purely insular objectives. Indeed the experience of a shrinking world and the inevitable exposure to a wide variety of factors has ensured that people from every walk of life participate in and search for best-practice solutions to the difficulties inherent in the need to share society with other cultures.

In the global village that we inhabit distances have apparently shrunk until one is able to wake at sunrise in one country and witness sunset in another country, even on another continent. Shared aspirations, interests and concerns are now so intertwined that momentous events in one country invariably affect neighbours and communities very far away. No problem develops without its implications being experienced across all the different layers of society, across national and supranational boundaries and through many diverse social networks, technological or otherwise.

And yet very few appear to possess the will or inclination to genuinely want to engage on issues of universal concern and join in genuine dialogue, so that the very concept of coexistence appears as something strange. It is as if the collective experience of life made possible on one level by the forces of social and technological progress has, on another level, alienated humankind, leaving only idealised, often impractical and almost always competing versions of countless *"isms"*. Instead of unity there is schism, in place of sincere dialogue, only indifference or undisguised antipathy.

Of paramount importance is the need to promote the basic principles of Islam, at the same time projecting its authentic culture, especially its

Muhammadan aspect. The present era of globalisation and consequent collision of cultures has brought into focus numerous concerns surrounding coexistence for those who adhere to Islam, with an urgent need for us to recognise and enter into dialogue with each other.

Globalisation need not alarm us as it represents an opportunity to build bridges within communities. Muslims who have migrated to the West can continue to make beneficial socio-economic and cultural contributions, whether in trade, sciences or the arts. Anxieties about globalisation are futile, not least because globalisation is a reality. What is needed now is sincere engagement with this reality, with an awareness of those aspects of globalisation, which may cause a fear of loss of identity. Retrieving Islam's established principles and authentic culture will surely help here. Like all true values sought and cherished by humanity, Islam's true values always resist distortions from within and without, and, just as often, shine even more brightly in moments of stress. This authentic culture is the most highly regarded within Islam but the least represented in the world at large. It is indeed represented by the life of the Prophet Muhammad who bequeathed a legacy of kindness in the form of freedom and justice, tolerance and harmonious coexistence.

Anxieties pertaining to coexistence can no longer be left unattended, subject only to personal experience, or glossed over by insincere proclamations. In distancing ourselves from the errors of the past, errors that have been exacerbated by mutual recrimination and antipathy between this or that faction, we must take care to retrieve the essential principles of Islam and re-enact these in practical terms in our lives. Laudatory texts and well-meaning organisations are all very well but experience is incomplete without practice so we are left with only so many good intentions and even where there is some effort it is doomed to failure because it is not based on fundamental principles. To retrieve the values that were translated into practical reality and the manner in which this was done, we have with us at all times the greatest exemplar of all, the Prophet. Asked about the Prophet's character, the Lady 'Aisha, replied, "His character was the Qur'an."[18]

For Muslims, the lament over past glories and golden ages has been with us for too long. History does not necessarily mean archived records. We would do well to consider that history might be a continuous process and we must therefore reaffirm the theory of coexistence, consummated through practice. The task at hand is to engage with the present in order to create the future by learning from, not lamenting, the past. Reviving these underlying principles will liberate Muslims, enabling them to contribute once more to the world rather than seeing themselves as marginalised and suffering internal feelings of shared desperation.

The Holy Prophet said, "Make things easy for the people, do not make things difficult for them, and give them good tidings and do not repulse them."[19] It is worth pausing and reflecting on what this asks of us. We are asked to be flexible not rigid and to use the power of our imaginations rather than turn to unthinking violence.

The Meaning of Muhammad and Our Cultural Memory

Fig 7: (In Diwani script), "I am sent only to perfect manners and morals." When faithful to the Prophet's example, Islam is a living culture emitting light unto nations

A common humanity; Against all unholy alliances

Questions of humanity, humanism and even whether there is such a thing definable as a human being have always been debated by thinkers, both ancient and modern. These are questions that acquire urgency in moments of stress. The conventional worldview of religious traditions, albeit with divergences between and sometimes within them, holds that God has brought into being a creation invested with an angelic nature and yet curiously prone to lapse at the same time. The human being, as conceived in the Islamic tradition, occupies the best of both worlds. That is, both the spiritual and the material.

Infused with the attributes of the Creator, the human being, when faithful to these god-like qualities, is able to rise higher than even the angels and God has endowed the human species as a whole with an elevated dignity far above the rest of His Creation. Thus the dignity of Man, together with a humanism based on God are in fact central to Islam. If the Qur'an is communicable to all humanity, it is because "the human" is central in a divinely-ordered universe. Religious orthodoxy and secular humanism would both discover comfortable accommodation in Islam, for the Qur'an provides direct expression of the primacy of the human being: *"Now, indeed, We have conferred dignity on the children of Adam, and borne them over land and sea, and provided for them sustenance out of the good things of life, and favoured them far above most of Our Creation."*[20]

Far from being left to sink or swim in a cosmos without meaning – the idea that has generated philosophical justifications for a "struggle for existence" – the human being is a cherished being with great meaning and worth. This verse alone is full of meaning, making explicit Man's status in Creation, the dispersal of the human race across all habitable environments and his inherent propensity for goodness. And the dignity and distinction conferred upon mankind encompasses all the children of Adam, without discrimination on grounds of belief, persuasion, colour or race in every time and place. Might it not be that that over-confident rationalisation has given philosophical respectability to discrimination and the construction of hierarchies? Notions of a universe in free-play have generated narratives of a general struggle for survival, thereby legitimising conflict, tribal and national rivalries, notions of racial superiority and wars of extermination.

Speaking from within a tradition appears problematic when that tradition is seen to be discredited, when tarred with the brush of intolerance, conflict and disharmony. We have discussed elsewhere the yawning gulf between representation and reality and yet if Islam is misrepresented externally and convulsed by distortion from within we nonetheless remain persuaded by the inherent mercy in Islam and its true principles. One such principle is recognition of the unity of the human race and the equality of all human beings.

From a God-centric view, one that recognises both goodness and fallibility in mankind, differentiation in the human family is measured only in terms of goodness and integrity, not in terms of racial or sectarian identity. Thus God says in the Qur'an, *"O humankind! Behold, We have created you all out of a male and a female, and have made you into nations and tribes, so that you might come to know one another. Verily, the noblest of you in the sight of God is the one most righteous. Behold, God is all-knowing, all-aware."*[21]

That humans have evolved and dispersed into nations and tribes does not undermine the unity of the human family nor its equality in biological origin, a proposition maintained by the Prophet Muhammad throughout his life. The essential oneness of mankind was the core theme in his famous farewell speech and he exhorted those privileged to hear it to spread the message. The Prophet's appeal to humanity and the response to it are timeless reminders that human freedom and equality are inviolable and sacrosanct:

"O people! Know indeed that your Lord is one, and that your Father is one. Indeed, there is not superiority in the Arab over the non-Arab nor is there superiority in the non-Arab over the Arab. There is not superiority in the white over the black nor is there superiority in the black over the white, except in righteousness. Have I, then, conveyed the Message?" The people replied: *"The Messenger of God has conveyed the message."* ... *"God has made sacred your money and your blood. Have I conveyed the message?" The people answered: "The Messenger of God has conveyed the message. Behold, the nearer ones of you should convey the message to the remoter ones."* [22]

In all our social relations, whether between individuals or between communities, between the individual and the state or between state and state, the basic demands of common values are rooted in humankind's essential oneness. Religious identity may be fractured and political opinion divided but humanism in the Islamic expression insists on equality of life and dignity of the individual and coexistence in harmony between all nations and their social layers.

The principle of unity in diversity, therefore necessarily entails harmonious coexistence in the cosmic order. Humankind in its composition and habitation is a microcosm of this cosmic order operating on justice, the chief principle by which harmony and cooperation is ensured. Equitable coexistence thus cannot be achieved in the absence of justice. For this reason the prophets of earlier times always spoke of justice and called on the people to act with kindness and to help each other.

If now we are experiencing individualism and national interest, or the adversarial positions implied by differences of class and gender, surely the prophets spoke rightly after all. Secular law and divine law both claim justice but, while secular law is governed by national interest, which automatically means certain individuals and certain courses of action have to be excluded, divine law, however, in appealing to a nobler aim, upholds the fundamental pillars of justice by encouraging us to love, feel for and co-operate with our fellow beings, in other words to be human in the fullest sense of that word.

Loyalty to nation, tribe or language group or the preservation of heritage and traditions are all traits inherent in mankind and humanism. Islam recognises and even recommends such affiliations. Diversity in heritage and tradition enables human beings to make personal contact and share knowledge, for we are always curious to experience the customs of others, to recognise and receive the marks of civility and kindness as the Qur'an reminds us, "And have made you into nations and tribes, so that you might come to know one another".

Here we learn the layered meaning of recognition. "Coming to know one another" means so much more than simply tolerating each other and implies an acceptance based on true understanding. Rejection, then, is the manifestation of self-interest and ignorance, a wilful failure to know one another. Intolerance thereby breeds malice and prejudice which, once sown, may be perpetuated down the generations.

Human history is dotted with the dark blots of conflict from wars fuelled by tribal and sectarian fanaticism. In the past these conflicts had much to do with the wars of princes and were sometimes fought under the cover of religion but even the modern era has witnessed two world wars with unspeakable destruction, instigated by supposedly enlightened nations. Claims of national destiny and the greater glory of tribe or god, or of civilization and culture, have provided sanctimonious cover for a host of malevolent enterprises, for instance territorial expansion, subjugation and exploitation of human and natural resources and military adventures in the name of moral superiority. Even when the sense of moral force may be justifiable, on humanitarian grounds for example, powerful nations blinded by their own arrogance employ unjustifiable methods. Fantasies of tribal honour and glory, so often the *casus belli* - cause of war - in the past, have been replaced by the grand claims of the guardians of world peace. However the pages of these latter fictions are also stained with blood.

The first years of the 21st century have passed in much the same way as the 20th century began and ended with terrible wars and humanitarian disasters in many parts of the globe. Millions of lives have been lost in internecine conflicts, more often than not sustained by a malevolent alliance of race, religion and economic interest. While this evil alliance is seemingly always at work in the Middle East, military adventurism in other parts of the globe is often explicitly in the aims of vested national interests and geopolitical power-play. The redrawing of borders and shifts in influence that attend such conflicts are almost always determined by economic and security needs, although the earth's resources are enough to sustain a responsible humankind. The Sustainer is well able to sustain His creation and our planetary existence is certainly within His knowledge: *"Does He not know – He Who has created? Indeed, He alone is unfathomable, all-aware!"*[23]

The unholy alliance of race, religion and economic interest practically drives modern conflict. Where antagonism is driven by racial tension alone, the end-result is as catastrophic as any other motive. The atrocities witnessed in former Yugoslavia, Rwanda, Burundi, Sri Lanka, Myanmar and elsewhere demonstrate how widespread the disease of racism is. Racial and cultural differences are, of course, not unimportant markers of identity and sense of being, that allow an individual to say, "this is my background" or a community to say, "this is our way". These identities have histories with their material and symbolic effects and the past will always speak to the present. But such identifications are also unstable, made and re-made through memory, experience, environment, narrative and social contract.

Those who employ the politics of race and culture are therefore always on unstable ground since racial and cultural identifications are always subject to history and undergoing perpetual transformation. This concept of identity and culture as a transformative positioning is always embraced by Islam, for God says: *"Had God so willed, He could surely have made you all one single community; however, He lets go astray him that wills to go astray and guides aright him that wills to be guided..."*[24] The verse just cited is properly related to ethical and moral values but it also enables us to accept transformations relevant to human communities, not least because the Divine Message addresses all mankind. For humankind, differences will persist but globalisation has also brought together diverse cultures and for this reason, too, it is ever more necessary for us to exercise some imaginative reunification and reaffirmation of our shared humanity.

Since religion claims to support justice by encouraging us to understand and identify with each other and so carry out the commandments that God has given us, it is shameful to see that so much strife has been caused by religious conflict. In the past and in the present powerful bodies have used religion as a disguise to conceal their true motives when killing innocent people and even slaughtering entire populations. Race, religion and economic interests are given priority over finding peaceful solutions to social problems. That does not mean that the teachings of Muhammad, Jesus, or Moses, are to blame or that the words passed down from Buddha or Confucius are wrong or that any particular belief should be held responsible for the acts of a few irresponsible or unrepresentative individuals. As mentioned, the principle of unity in diversity, so fundamental to Islam, naturally embraces the idea of harmonious co-existence in the cosmic order. In its recognition of common human origins as well as difference, Islamic humanism is therefore inseparable from the idea of people of different beliefs and cultural backgrounds living together harmoniously as part of a modern civilisation.

Islamic tradition, then, is not so easily discredited, however much it has been tarred with the brush of intolerance, conflict and disharmony. Appearances and reality may not always match, but in the recognition of human biological unity and natural equality there is an inherent mercy that makes the true culture of Islam the ideal expression and style for modern societies.

It is perhaps as easy to speak of a silent majority as it is to condemn the obviously unrepresentative minority, but there is an urgent need for recognition that there is, indeed, a true culture of Islam. Approached without bias or distortion, the Qur'an and the Prophetic Paradigm stand as eternal foils to the darkness projected on Islam. This authentic culture is not to be found through the mass media illustrated with lurid images nor in the widely circulated and distorted Islamic literature. It is when we are truly faithful to the authentic tradition that Islam will become a living culture once again emitting light unto nations. It is the Islam of the Holy Prophet that extinguished the fire of racism, demonstrated how to replace discord with harmony and levelled difference of class, tribe and gender. Once the Holy Prophet was in a reclining position but stood up as a mark of respect for a Jewish funeral cortege. Asked about his action, he replied: "Isn't it a human soul?"[25]

Overlooking stalwart members from among his own Makkan community as well as the men of Madinah who had hastened to shelter him, he handpicked Bilal the Abyssinian to be his *muezzin*. "...Verily, the noblest of you in the sight of God is the one best in conduct. Behold, God is all-knowing, all-aware".[26] In appointing Bilal, a former slave, the Holy Prophet thus set down a template for a meritocracy, simultaneously obliterating nepotism and distinctions of class and colour. Bilal's appointment as the one to call to prayer holds special significance on many levels. The Holy Prophet emphasized the spiritual importance of the *muezzin's* venerable position, saying: "*Muezzins* will have longer necks on the Day of Resurrection."[27]

Such a radical break came not without strain. When Bilal was slighted by his contemporary, Abu Dhar, the latter, was put in his place with joking words that he, too, showed traces of darkness.[28] Yet in material terms and in the context of seventh Century Arabia, Bilal's elevation from bondage to pre-eminence was a stunning triumph over race, colour and class. The dominant culture in our contemporary world is able to celebrate the elevation of a black man to the highest executive power, and rightly so, but it is also true that there was a light beamed fifteen centuries earlier by Islam. And if our world has suffered from the decline of civilization-in-Islam,[29] the human world can overcome its conflicts and injustices by once more looking to the example of the Prophet Muhammad.

When a quarrel erupted between the Madinan tribes of Aws and the Khazraj, the Holy Prophet quelled their dispute with a direct appeal to enlightened thought: "By God, do you propagate ignorance whilst I am among you? After God has guided you to Islam, honoured you, dispelled ignorance and united you?"[30] Here is the classic example of innate goodness, which although it is threatened by ignorance, can be overcome by an appeal to expansive thought and nobler aims. Since sectarian rivalry and intolerance are equated with barbarity and ignorance, it is something that continues to divide and blight Muslims. However an appeal to unity comes from the greatest source and it is unequivocal: "He who propagates tribalism is not from among us, he who fights on the basis of tribalism is not from among us, and he who dies for tribalism is not from among us."[31] Enlightened minds thereby shun sectarianism in all its forms and we are urged to "abandon it, for it is rotten".[32]

Fig 8: (In Diwani script), "...Behold, thou [O Muhammad] keepest indeed to a sublime way of life." The Prophet Muhammad, – on him peace and blessings, – bequeathed a legacy of freedom and justice, tolerance and harmonious coexistence, but Islam's authentic culture is the least represented

An elevated individual; A true ornament of civilization

We human beings know the history of our kind by reflecting on our own achievements in social, political and cultural development, even as we compare and scrutinise past civilizations through their architectural, scientificand cultural legacies. As important markers of historical epochs and periods, these monuments of past civilizations cause us to marvel at them, but they also serve as material for study for scholars and thinkers who hold up the past as a mirror to contrast and compare with our own claims to progress. Scientific and scholarly endeavour in this regard give cause for both excitement and sober reflection. Fresh discoveries or new meaning may infuse the common inheritors of past civilizations with pride, but the contours of human history should also check complacency, assumptions of ever-lasting power and overweening confidence in their modern equivalents.

Our efforts to explore and determine cause and effect, a process embraced by Islam, may turn on new meanings and re-imaginings and yet we cannot escape the existential conundrum of life, our purpose and the inexorability of decay and death. In fact the Qur'an demands reflection on the history of humankind and its long progress and also regressions, simultaneously offering sure guidance for individual and collective negotiation of our existence and lessons to draw upon. This is from Adam's genesis to the paths trodden by the many early human communities that were the seedbed of other civilizations that flowered and then withered over time.

For this reason the basis of mankind's religious and socio-cultural history – alongside monotheism and ethics – underlies the explanatory principles of Qur'anic study. As monotheism is intimately connected to the received wisdom about human origins and purpose, a topic that would otherwise necessitate an extensive monograph, it naturally demands brief discussion here. The theme of monotheism in Islam, insisting on God's Oneness, promotes the understanding that while absolute knowledge of God is beyond our understanding, He is yet comprehensible through His

Attributes, readable in Nature and proclaimed through Scripture. His Oneness, evident in unity and purpose, is reflected in His Attributes. The Qur'an itself draws attention to the limits of our knowledge: *"I called them not to witness the creation of the heavens and the earth, not even their own creation... "*[33] We might understand this axiom through a simple analogy. We retain basic information about our birth, in terms of place and time, but the "fact" of time and place is nonetheless knowledge received from others.

The Qur'an is quite explicit about the stress on human history. The triumphs and travails of, for example, the organic communities of Noah and the *'Aad* and the *'Thamud*, as well as the global civilizations of Egypt and the Greco-Roman worlds, even the seemingly obscure and yet rich heritage of *'Qataba* and Sheba, among others. In the context of the Qur'an this emphasis on human history encouraged a sense of caution, that warns against too-high assumptions about power and prestige. We are thereby encouraged to learn from and reflect on the progress of history and urged to remain aware of the significance of permanent struggle and to guard against decline.

The Qur'an is remarkably timeless in this regard: *"Have they, then, never journeyed about the earth and beheld what happened in the end to those who lived before their time? Greater were they in power than they are; and they left a stronger impact on the earth, and built it up even more than these. And to them came their apostles with all evidence of the truth. And so it was not God who wronged them, but it was they who had wronged themselves. "*[34] Given that the civilizations of the past projected such power and influence, their legacies were always bound to survive in one form or another and posterity is able to trace and marvel at these achievements. For some, a focus on the arts, architecture, prose and poetry, music and sculpture was important. Yet others, concentrated on the development of science and technological progress from medicine to enhanced public works and the rise of urban living.

What distinguishes civilization in Islam is the emphasis placed on the development of the individual. That is not to say that Islamic civilization neglected what its predecessors had done. It, too, played its part in skill and invention, prescription of law and maintenance of order, the raising of cities and wealth-creation. But the civilization stimulated by Islam also conceived its purpose as two-fold, sowing for harvests yet to come. For the law-givers and banishers of falsehoods also took great care to ensure the progress of humanity and the environment necessary to its development.

Libraries and centres of learning held far more prestige than the grandest mosque or the most imposing palace, so that knowledge and understanding were placed at the very heart of a civilization in which the individual and society were suffused with elevated thought in an environment upholding the highest ethics and practical morals. A civilization that produced some of the best in arts and sciences, remained conscious of the brevity of time, of the lessons of history, and therefore paid greater attention to humanity and to individual purpose. Such an anthropocentric worldview in turn motivated a still-higher aspiration - harmony with the Divine Attributes. For, if the highest ideals were the fruits of knowledge and understanding, these could only be experienced through virtuous action. The ruler of a vast empire and the commander of armies, the learned scholar and the humble worshipper, the eloquent poet and the wealthy trader might attain short-lived fame and riches but would gain immeasurably more through sincere action that benefited both himself and others. *"...And God's goodly acceptance is the greatest success; for this, this is the triumph supreme!"*[35] It was by means of such elevated thought, invariably matched by action, that civilization in Islam flourished. It is for this reason that we prefer to employ the term "civilization in Islam" and not "Islamic civilization". As an aside, it is a shameful fact that while Islam aims at the universal, even as it respects difference, the contemporary trend for labels is such that even water is now bottled as "Islamic". Still, the civilization that we speak of also encompassed non-Muslims who were persuaded by its ideals and found certainty in its promise of human emancipation and the release of individual potential. Steadfastly refusing narrow definitions, Islam continues to embrace the idea of *"a mercy unto the worlds"*. Indeed, one might say that the emphasis on human development, aspiring to the highest ideals of compassion and generosity, to name but two of the Divine Attributes, and not the relative size and strength of nations, trade surplus or military prowess, is what makes human beings civilized.

The primacy of knowledge and learning, then, is the distinguishing marker of civilization in Islam and striving-after human development is its ultimate objective (not for want of trying, if not always realised). It should not therefore surprise us that the very first Qur'an verses revealed to the Prophet commanded him to *"Read, in the name of thy Sustainer, Who has created. Created man out of a germ-cell! Read, for thy Sustainer is the Most Bountiful One. Who has taught [man] the use of the Pen. Taught man what he did not know!"*[36] They remain wise sayings that speak to us down the centuries.

On arrival in Madinah, the Prophet sanctioned the building of a mosque, very much intended as the nucleus of all aspects of Muslim individual and social development and not as a narrowly-defined place of communal prayer. Many of the early Muslims in both Makkah, where the verses commanding adherents to read had been revealed, and in Madinah could barely relate to use of the pen. Very early on, the Prophet determined that the prime structural task of Islam was individual development grounded in holistic education and expansive learning. He thus taught his companions that mosque construction was a functional affair, not an enterprise that should take up much time or expense, instructing them to *"erect a pole, like the pole of Moses"*,[37] meaning that the worshipper who connects and communes with God is more important than the building in which he prays.

The teaching of such values not only affirmed the intimate relationship between God and the worshipper but emphasised the high ideals aimed at in Islam, ideals that promote individual emotions over mere form and function so that the enlightened human being rather than the sacred building becomes the enduring ornament of civilisation. From the very first revelation, the Prophet started a revolution of the human mind that would in time extend way beyond Arabian society and culture. In fact what the Prophet did was to fill his listeners with a deep-seated realisation of the high regard that the individual is capable of feeling for the Creator and he further underlined the privileged closeness between Creator and all created beings with the emphatic statement, *"The whole earth is made for me a mosque and sanctified."*[38]

Veneration of any symbol of the Divine was to be praised but Islam would have no interest in meaningless pomp and grandeur and the true temple of worship would reside in the heart of the worshipper. The measure of achievement in Islam was to be the gradual raising up of humanity, not the construction of impressive buildings and monuments.

Only those whose concern is with labels may mourn the end of Islamic civilization with the glittering decadence of Abbasid rule or the end of this or that caliphate, but as long as individuals concentrate on their own personal improvement, civilization in Islam remains an ideal to aim for. Of course, civilization in Islam, for all its high ideals, was not safe from errors and backsliding, drawing on itself the comforting cliché, *"to err is to be human"*.

Muslims cannot grow weary of carrying the banner of humanity, not if they are true to their purpose, for Islam values the human being as the most privileged of God's creatures: *"Now, indeed, have We conferred dignity on the children of Adam, and borne them over land and sea, and provided for them sustenance out of the good things of life, and favoured them far above most of Our Creation.* " [39] Islam will have no dealing with dogmas that saddle the human with the weight of despair or explain our existence as a lottery; rather, civilization in Islam instils hope and gives meaning to life by welcoming the high honour of being granted superior intellect and agency. *"He it is Who has made the earth easy to live upon: go about, then, in all its regions, and partake of the sustenance which He provides; but unto Him you shall be resurrected."*[40]

If the human being enters this world as no more than a cell, he or she is still valued right from the beginning, for God tells us far more about our identity and origins than the bare information of place and date offered by the birth certificate. *"And when We told the angels, 'Prostrate yourselves before Adam!', they all prostrated themselves... "*[41] Such high honour from the very beginning and our privileged position in this world do not come without responsibility since the process of civilizing and refining that we call elevated individual thought and intellect also mirrors the growth from cell to fully developed human being. And having been granted the means to make the most of our time in this world, we are responsible and accountable on many levels for the choices that we make, since our connection or severance from our Sustainer for our treatment of our fellow human beings or of the animals under our command and for the efficient use or mismanagement of the entire universe are noted by our Creator. It is a responsibility that we can neither throw off nor regard as something imposed upon us, but one that we must welcome in the secure knowledge of our exalted origin and purpose: *"Know, then, that there is no god but God."*[42]

Masses of conflicting ideas and the babbling isms that they generate may vanish like the legendary Tower of Babel, but the cherishing and generous One who guides us aims at our continued enlightenment, encouraging us to appreciate the value of knowledge and understanding above all other human achievements. *"...And God will exalt by many degrees those of you*

who have attained to faith and such as have been vouchsafed knowledge. "[43]
This is a secure promise and the most eloquent expression of what
civilization in Islam entails.

God, it seems, has been cherishing humanity in this way all along, from His
teaching Adam *"the names of all things",*[44] meaning the ability to
understand and discriminate, the ability to choose and the further special
distinction of the human being to form conceptual thought. Since
discrimination may result in a flawed choice or a momentary lapse, as
Adam soon discovered, God in His generosity granted humanity the
prophets, to be their guiding lights and for their continuing education and
for the support of their tribes, nations and civilizations. It is no coincidence
that the advent of the greatest educator of all, Muhammad, came at the
point of humanity's first tentative steps towards the Information Age that is
our inheritance. To act as guide and shepherd was, of course, the anointed
role of all apostles and emissaries but Muhammad placed teaching and
learning at the very heart of his mission. Always quick to respond with
mercy, no matter what the circumstances, the Prophet seized just such an
opportunity on the battlefield at *Badr*. With his principal companions
suggesting various solutions to the fates of Makkan captives (arguments
ranged from customary ransom to on-the-spot-executions) the Prophet
intervened to set his own terms. The lives of all of the captives would be
spared, the wealthiest among them would be offered for ransom but the
poorer among them had something far greater to offer the fledgling Muslim
community; each captive Makkan would be obliged to teach ten of his
Muslim captors how to read and write – and that intervention was in fact
the Muslims' very first experience of literacy. We might at this point break
off to consider the huge difference between the "jihadists" in our time and
the Muslims after Badr. Many of the Makkan prisoners joined the Muslim
community, so impressed were they by the behaviour and ethics of those
who held them captive.

The self-satisfied view of Islam's culture as all law and punishment, rules and regulations, simply fails to grasp the true meaning of the civilizing mission which the Prophet based on knowledge and learning. The convoluted relationship between moral obligation and legal duty should not concern us here but we are reminded of the heavy emphasis the Prophet placed on enlightenment through education: *"Seeking knowledge is obligatory for every Muslim."*[45] And on a more expansive note:

"What is the matter with people that they do not teach their neighbours, nor make them aware, nor encourage them to do good, nor forbid wrongdoing? And what is the matter with people who do not learn from their neighbours? By God, people are expected to teach their neighbours and make them aware and encourage and admonish, and people are expected to learn from their neighbours, or punishment will fall on them in this world."[46]

Here in fact is the authentic voice of Islam, far removed from the thunderous sounds associated with biblical traditions. The Prophet was ever-mindful of his own role as the last of the guiding lights and his concern was to add his own spirit of care and compassion to common morality. Here we find the *"Seal of the Prophets"* intent on spreading his message so as to bring about the advancement of society through civilizing values. He does not threaten punishment in an after-world but warns against paying for wrong-doing in this present world, and by wrong-doing he means the falling away of humanity, the slide back into barbarism, into darkness. More meanings surface when read at the same time as the Qur'anic history-lesson to *"...behold what happened in the end to those who lived before their time...it was not God who wronged them, but it was they who had wronged themselves"*. It is not brimstone and thunderbolts from Heaven that threaten humanity with punishment in this world, rather it is mankind's tendency towards moral decay and self-destruction. Instead of neighbourliness, friendly relations and dialogue, we have class struggle and social inequality rooted in a lack of education and civic rights, corporate greed and economic depression, the ever-present danger of international conflict and the threat of ecological destruction. The Prophet knew that there would not be another light after him to guide humanity, so he and his teaching would have to illuminate the world.

So civilization in Islam means enabling the individual to fulfil his destiny by maintaining harmony in the universe, for all Creation is attuned to this harmony: *"The Heavens extol His limitless Glory, and the earth, and all that they contain; and there is not a single thing but extols His limitless Glory and praise: but you fail to grasp the manner of their glorifying Him! Verily, He is forbearing, much-forgiving!"*[47] His loving care of the human race has been there all along, sustaining and guiding humanity towards goodness, which is synonymous with civilization. The civilized human being will then feel and demonstrate concern for every creature in this vast ecology, extending kindness to fellow human beings as well as to all other organisms great and small, wild or domesticated. Contemporary thinking is apt to imagine that animal rights follow from human rights and are the outcome of distinctly modern legislative measures. This is certainly true to some extent and yet as long as fifteen-hundred years ago the Prophet famously enjoyed close relations with animals, including pet-names for his camel and horse. It is also true that he once corrected a woman who deprived a pet cat of food,[48] and praised a man who had provided a thirsty dog with drinking water.[49]

Such good behaviour extends to conscious and unconscious parts of the universe, although our conceptions of what constitute apparently living or conscious creatures are quite limited in light of God's declaration that *"the Heavens extol His limitless glory...but you fail to grasp the manner of their glorifying Him"*. Long before our own modern concerns about environmental damage through heavy industry, about climate control, depleted fish stocks in the world's oceans or even the scarcity of water, we

find the Prophet, proclaiming, *"Whosoever revives a dead land, it is his."*[50]
A proclamation of this kind might appear problematic when we are
reminded of the unconvincing excuses advanced by colonisers in the recent
past or modern corporate greed. In the context of the 7th Century,
however, in the drought-prone oases and dry deserts of Arabia, such a call
to make productive use of natural resources held social value as much as
individual gain. These are among the ideal characteristics of "civilized
Man" promoted by Islam, and these are the achievements and also the as
yet unachieved aims of civilization in Islam.

When civilization in Islam was solely centred on raising Man's stature the
first recipients of the civilizing experience of revelation migrated from the
Arabian Peninsula to spread the message and enlighten others and the rapid
and long-lasting success they achieved in this undertaking was due entirely
to their civilized conduct.

Known as Muslims, these migrants crossed frontiers as liberators,
emancipating tribes and nations from slavery, injustice and tyranny.
Instead of the fire and sword carried by traditional conquerors they touched
lives with care and compassion and raised high the torch of learning in the
most distant lands. Muhammad al-Bukhari, whose *Sahih* collection is a
byword for Hadith scholarship, virtually put Bukhara in central Asia on the
map. Sibawayh, himself a Persian, standardised Arabic grammar and most
of the students of Abdullah Ibn Abbas, one of Islam's leading early
scholars, were the children of freed slaves.

If all nations in Islam, irrespective of caste, colour or creed, enjoyed the
trappings of "civilization", it was because the New Man, that is Civilized
Man, had nobler aims than mere personal enrichment or national
aggrandizement. History tells us that the material wealth of the lands under
the sway of Islam remained intact and in certain situations increased, but
the Arabian Peninsula remained an unusually sleepy collection of oases,

including Madinah its spiritual home, and placid market towns including the focal point of worship, Makkah. The twin centres of Islam never housed imperial palaces or armed garrisons, nor attracted journeymen and adventurers.

Muslim rule extended across the vast continent of India, yet Islam still remains a minority religion in that country. Christians and Jews fled a Europe dominated by an all-encompassing Papal regime, a backwater of feuding princes and robber barons, seeking refuge and the best of higher learning in Muslim Spain and North Africa and later paving the way for Europe's own Enlightenment. Civilization in Islam was not without its fair share of pomp and pageantry and had its own sophisticated state institutions, public services and the high standards of living associated with that level of development. Above all, civilization in Islam was synonymous with the flowering of art and science, it was not only the wonder of its own time but the precursor of our world today. Topkapi and the Taj Mahal are the world's heritage and rightly so. They certainly cannot be claimed as exclusively Islamic. Rather the absolute importance of education and learning was the mark of Civilized Man, who in turn is the as-yet incomplete achievement of Islamic civilization.

Discussion of ethical values becomes unnecessary where the individual is installed at the heart of a God-centric universe. Human development and self-realization are the aims of Civilization in Islam, yet we must conclude with a brief remark related to this and also with reference to our past, present and future. The raising up of the individual is the recipe for human happiness because knowledge of our origin gives meaning to, and hope for, our present and future states.

We may struggle to grasp that feeble human beings started life as the objects of angelic reverence in a higher realm but an awareness of God's love and watchful care and our own destiny should prompt gratitude and an appropriate appreciation on our part. God certainly provides more answers than our own birth certificates or the theories of those who disbelieve in Him. As they say, *"How could it be, that He who has created all should not know all? He alone is unfathomable, all- aware!"*[51] The Creator, to whom we trace our origins, therefore knows what is good for us and He granted us absolute choice when He provided us with the abilities to think and reason. Furthermore, He sent guiding lights, one after another, across the span and history of our species, showing us the right path, the path that enables us to rise above ourselves. But not only guiding lights, He has also extended to us a direct line of communication so that we are never alone, never without connection, in our appeal, *"Guide us to the straight path."*[52] Should we forget the teachings of the guiding lights, the prophets, or fail to connect by asking Him directly, then that very ability to reason with which He has equipped us enables us to know Him and His daily and hourly working in the universe. That, and the oft-repeated lessons of history, awaken our consciousness and sense of purpose. In His words: *"O you who have attained to faith! Remain conscious of God; and let every human being look to what he sends ahead for the morrow! And again, remain conscious of God, for God is fully aware of all that you do. And be not like those who are oblivious of God, and whom He therefore causes to be oblivious of their own selves: it is they, they who are truly debased!"*[53]

Fig 9: (In Musalsal and Diwani), "Spread peace among yourselves, give away food to the needy, pray while people sleep and you shall enter Paradise, the house of peace."

The humanitarian: The Prophet's civilizing mission

Our universal notions of compassion and decency relate to the laws and institutions that serve mankind, whether spiritual or temporal, insofar as they cultivate innate goodness in humanity. The conventions of our societies may determine the nature of manners and morals and these may become obsolete with the passage of time but the principle of inherent goodness is as universal as it is timeless. Religion, as a regulating mechanism, functions to establish justice and to guide humanity to what is most virtuous while it highlights the unity of innate goodness through diversity.

In this regard, the Muslim belief in the essential unity of God's messengers is particularly illuminating. Central to the message of Islam is a belief in all divine emissaries and scriptures. Abraham, Moses, David and Jesus are all specifically mentioned as bearers of God's Word (although not all those messages are available to us other than by word of mouth). Others are mentioned as inheritors but, the Qur'an being the most universal form of the Divine Word, the distinguished list of emissaries is rounded off by Muhammad. The Qur'an thereby addresses universal humanity: *"Say, 'We believe in God, and in that which has been bestowed from on high upon us, and that which has been bestowed upon Abraham and Ishmael and Isaac and Jacob and their descendants, and that which has been vouchsafed to Moses and Jesus, and that which has been vouchsafed to all the prophets by their Sustainer; we make no distinction between any of them. And it is unto Him that we surrender ourselves.'"*[54]

While the centrality of God's oneness runs like a red thread through all Divine messages, the attention to individual and social responsibility is amplified in the Qur'an, the Hadith and other respected writing. *"And remember! We accepted this solemn pledge from the children of Israel: 'You shall worship none but God; and you shall do good unto your parents and kinsfolk, and the orphans, and the poor; and you shall speak unto all people in a kindly way..."*[55] By emphasising the whole of the "children of

75

Israel", the verse just cited draws attention to both Torah and Gospel and the shared testimony of earlier traditions to uphold and spread humane ideals.

The Prophet Muhammad in his own teachings emphasised the essential connections between all the apostles and their missions: *"I am the nearest to Jesus, son of Mary, in this world and in the next, for all prophets are brothers on their father's side and share the same religion, and there has been no prophet between me and Jesus."*[56] And, like his brother prophets before him, the last of God's messengers also endorsed personal and civic responsibilities, saying, *"I am sent only to perfect manners and morals."*[57]

The concepts of good morals and humane behaviour are part and parcel of the worship of God as evidenced by the demands made on the newest recipients of the Divine Writ and the reminder to older recipients. Doing good to one's own *"parents and kinsfolk"* as well as to the dispossessed in society, *"the orphans and the poor"*, and good communication, including the ideal of peaceful coexistence, are therefore inseparable from the awareness of God. In the memorable Qur'an verse enjoining the ritual fast God reveals, *"O you who have attained to faith, fasting is ordained for you as it was ordained for those before you, so that you might remain conscious of God"*[58] Jesus is famously abstemious in older religious literature as well as in the literature of Islam, but in the Qur'an we find that his self-denial conjoins prayer and alms-giving, thereby underlining the equal importance of self-realisation through worship, of which fasting is the highest form, charity, compassionate care, and graceful conduct, *"And He has made me blessed wherever I may be; and He has enjoined upon me prayer and charity as long as I live. And He has endowed me with piety towards my mother; and He has not made me haughty or bereft of grace."*[59]

The shared traditions of worship and the pledge to benefit mankind mean that Islam, Christianity and Judaism have always been in conversation together and this is a dialogue that cannot be broken off. The need for dialogue is even greater in the face of the myriad challenges to peaceful coexistence and social harmony in our world today. These challenges are not only related to long-standing disputes about religion, race and nationality but also relate to the competition between generations, the so-called battle of the sexes, insecurities of gender and identity, to name but a few.

Muslims share with other monotheistic believers a common fount from which spring universal principles, for the Qur'an reveals a relationship conceived and perfected in a primordial realm, *"And indeed! We did accept a solemn pledge from all the prophets – from thee [O Muhammad], as well as from Noah and Abraham and Moses and Jesus the son of Mary; for We accepted a most solemn, weighty pledge from all of them; so that He might ask those men of truth as to [what response] their truthfulness [received on earth]..."*[60]

As each of these prophets was to become a guiding force of human societies, in many cases as tribal patriarch and common ancestor of later communities, their collective pledge to convey the Divine Message was always sensitive to time, place and audience. While the messengers did indeed guide to the truth, by implication we, too, are obliged to uphold the Divine Writ, to *"perfect manners and morals"*. The ways and means may be conditioned by time and place but all the principles that pertain to good morals and humane conduct are universal.

Shifts in thought and behaviour are undeniably the cause of variation in environment and therefore social interaction necessitates sensitivity and the consideration of others' psycho-social conditions, best expressed by the formula *"you shall speak unto all people in a kindly way"*. Thunderous sermons from pulpit or *mimbar*, threatening fire and brimstone on a society that has lost its moral compass, might once have been fashionable in particular settings though its efficacy is debatable, but human beings respond far better to reason and humane advances that follow the rule to *"speak unto all people in a kindly way"*.

In this regard it is well worth remembering that if the Prophet Muhammad defined his mission as the perfection of morals and manners he certainly achieved his intention and to a superlative degree. Where others variously distinguished between Jew and Gentile, freedman and slave, cleric and layman, man and woman, the message of the Prophet is an address to all humanity, embracing, in fact, all of our conceptions about the known universe: *"And We have sent thee as a kindness to all the worlds."*[61] While the content of the message is obviously universal, one aspect of its dissemination, the Messenger's living example, is greatly instructive. He patiently received and taught Revelation and just as patiently explained the purpose of his mission, literally winning over a great many with his smile, and a great many others through simple patience.

If the thematic and formal properties of Qur'an revelation awed follower and opponent alike, its duration, the 23 years of the Prophet's ministry, and gradual disclosure allowed for easy learning and an enduring result. The Qur'an itself draws attention to the process:

"A discourse which We have gradually unfolded, so that thou might read it out to mankind by stages, seeing that We have bestowed it from on high step by step, as one revelation."[62] The point, of course, is that even the best discourse, whether glad tidings of a happy afterlife or urgings to generous solutions and fair dealings in society, will always find a responsive audience and leave a lasting impression if the approach is friendly and generous. For that very reason, the Prophet's example remains the indispensable model. When God praises the Prophet He praises his timeless example, *"Even as We have sent unto you an apostle from among yourselves to convey unto you Our messages, and to cause you to grow in*

purity, and to impart unto you revelation and wisdom, and to teach you that which you knew not."[63]

Embodying wisdom, patience, justice, ardent sincerity, courage and generosity, the Prophet was tireless in his efforts to remedy social discontent, correct misconceptions and spread universal ethics even when these found expression in other sources. In this he was true to his promise, that he was *"come to perfect"*, the very expression revealing his own deep humility and recognition of the contribution of his brother prophets.

The Qur'an itself insists that it is a confirmation of what came before and that the Prophet is the last complete role model. God confirms his function *"Verily, in the Apostle of God you have a good example for everyone who looks forward to God and the Last Day, and remembers God unceasingly."*[64] As the perfect example for humanity the Prophet is the template for all times until *"the Last Day"* and following the Prophetic Paradigm is no less than the measure of God-consciousness *"and remembers God unceasingly"*. Translated into lived experience, what defines the Prophetic Paradigm is the Prophet's fusion of a moral standard that is above all humane and universal with ethical principles laid down in the Qur'an which, broadly speaking, aim at justice and equality, social cohesion and good governance.

The Prophet's virtuous conduct was in fact part of his character from his earliest years since he was already celebrated as *"Al Ameen"*, the Trusted One, in pre-Islamic Arab society. The Prophet's moral rectitude simply did not permit expediency, whether personal or political, so that the moral course is always the rational one. His being known as the Trusted One was confirmed by his refusal to favour any one interest group at the rebuilding of the Kaa'ba, while all the features of virtuous conduct were on display at once in his negotiation of the *Hudaybiyya* Treaty, steadiness, cool courage, temperance, sincere goodwill and generosity. If these qualities proclaim

God-consciousness, their tangible benefits in the here-and-now are peace and stability.

All the distinctions that we associate with the Prophet require superlatives in their own right but in relation to our present discussion it was the perfection of manners and morals in his own character and conduct that deserves special mention and certainly brought down on him the highest degree of praise, "...*Behold, thou [O Muhammad] keepest indeed to a sublime way of life.*"[65] Consistent with interpretations of the term *kuluq* in Arabic, *way of life* also encompasses shades of meanings that include *character* or *innate disposition* as well as the concept of *habitual behaviour* or *manner*. When asked about the Prophet's character, the simple reply of the Lady 'Aisha, stressed the same: "*His way of life was the Qur'an.*"[66]

Those who came into contact with him could not fail to be impressed by the Prophet's special traits, to the extent that in his own lifetime began the ripple effect of elevated thought, individual and social progress and universal enlightenment, a phenomenon we may broadly describe as civilization in Islam. The "coming to perfect manners and morals" is the humanitarian mission of Islam. Most obviously his companions, but also succeeding generations, basked in the honour, glory even, of civilization in Islam precisely because they took on those special characteristics left to them by the Prophet.

In one sense, the collection of the Qur'an, signalling the end of Revelation, announced that same perfection, but in another sense it set down the pattern for others to copy, a pattern that was always accessible and always discernible in the Prophet's own life. As God says, "*Say [O Prophet]: 'If you love God, follow me, God will love you and forgive you your sins; for God is much forgiving, a dispenser of grace.'*"[67] There is an additional set of meanings here. Moral standards may be overturned by a change of environment but fidelity to God will be measured by copying the one whose characteristics He has so exalted. Rather than weaken in faith the Prophet's example, synonymous with divine love, responds with patience and kindness.

In this way the Prophet's humanitarian mission not only caused a major change in social attitudes that we have elsewhere described as "global thinking", but as a root-and-branch project it also focused on personal development that aimed to raise mankind from animal instincts. As the basic unit of organised society, the elevated individual would inevitably produce a humane culture. In this way self-image would be dependant not on power over others but on self-control and the literature of Islam is full of the Prophet's moral teaching. *"The strong person is not the powerful wrestler. Rather, the strong person is the one that controls his anger"* he advised his followers according to Hadith tradition.[68]

In the same vein the Prophet warns against suspicion, which includes slander and baseless rumour, saying, *"Avoid suspicion for suspicion is the most false of talk,"*[69] and *"It is enough of a lie for a person to narrate everything that they hear."*[70] The larger point here is the Prophet's lumping together of individual and social conscience. Our supposedly modern assumptions about motives and impulses have produced conflicting analyses of psycho-social relations in the fields of gender, class, and both local and national sovereignty and yet the Prophet recognised that self control goes hand in hand with social harmony. He therefore warns against behaviour that tends towards violence: "The bankrupt will arrive on the Day of Resurrection with prayers, fasting and charity, but having also reviled others, spread falsehood, unlawfully devoured wealth, and attacked and shed blood of others. In recompense, the bankrupt's good deeds will be transferred to their victims. If good deeds are insufficient, the victims' poor deeds will be transferred to the bankrupt, and they will thereafter face severe recompense."[71]

These Traditions may be read in conjunction with the explicit warning in the Qur'an against the disruption to communal ties occasioned by suspicion or misrepresentation: *"...If any iniquitous person comes to you with a slanderous tale, use your discernment, lest you hurt people unwittingly and afterwards be filled with remorse for what you have done."*[72]

These are fragmentary insights into the ethical codes and moral guidelines that underpin Islam's humanitarian, civilizing mission, which is the foundation of all religious truth. Civilization in Islam, with its heightened focus on human development as the pivot of social progress, effectively shut out humanity's dark past and opened a future lit by the sun of freedom. The rays of this sun light up friendship, kindness, justice and tolerance and if this sun is momentarily eclipsed, we must nevertheless constantly attempt in our present actions to create a future world where that sun of freedom is always shining. We have the best of guides to lead us into that future, Muhammad, he who embraced all humanity and stretched out his hand to even the most unfriendly enemy.

God reminds us, *"Tell those who are bent on denying the truth that if they desist, all that is past shall be forgiven them."*[73] Our world is being shaped by a new age and we must answer the challenges that mark the crossing into that new age with those universal standards that first threw light upon the world in which we live.

Fig 10: (In Diwani script), "Be conscious of God wherever you are, and when you err be prepared to erase error through what is virtuous. And show to all mankind the best of character," said the Prophet Muhammad, – on him peace and blessings. Muslims, when Muhammadan in their cultural outlook, become "a mercy unto all the worlds"

A remedy for the suffering of the global village

The great challenges faced by mankind today in the social, political, economic and cultural fields threaten the very future of the human race. We say this in the full knowledge that such predictions usually provoke equally predictable replies. These tend to range from the something-must-be-done hand-wringing that rapidly descends into a game of blame-the-other-person, to the more common and cynical retort, *"But we've heard all this before."* Throughout the history of mankind, warnings about a collective car-crash have been answered with frustration, ridicule or outright hostility from all those who heard them.

In what we see as the far-off past, when the prophets of God regularly passed on such warnings, they normally received showers of sticks and stones by way of answers, often accompanied by a sarcastic request to bring it on! The last of God's messengers, Muhammad, and the most recent in memory, also had to put up with these taunts, stones thrown at him, a bloodied mouth and endless attempts to kill him. Responses like these never put off the earlier prophets, because they also had believers and followers who, once persuaded by their sincere speeches, took over the necessary responsibility. These people simply rolled up their sleeves and got on with whatever they were meant to be doing and did their work with friendliness and consideration for each other. Now, however, philosophers and sincere thinkers, those other preachers of Man's destiny, are scared of being laughed at as prophets of doom. Even when they do announce thoughtful analyses and the occasional stark warning, their voices are drowned by those who pass on lies and say only what is advantageous to themselves. These people often take on the role of policy gurus and peacemakers.

Social inequality and powerlessness, the fragmentation of society and the individual's feeling of being totally lost in the world of today, cultural battles and groups at war with each other, revolution and reaction, economic depression, ongoing wars and humanitarian disasters and the very real prospect of irreversible environmental damage are among the many problems we face at this moment. Some of these problems are historically deep-rooted while others appear to recur in cycles and only seem to be important because of our peculiar problem of forgetfulness and failure to learn the lessons of history. Our problem of amnesia is all the more bizarre considering the global flow of information brought about by modern technology. We might complain about the general lack of intention to deal with these various problems at a political level but, sadly, what is also absent is a collective sense of responsibility that might result in meaningful dialogue leading to genuine cooperation. Instead of making use of our new technology to communicate with each other and open up useful discourse, we allow the availability of instant up-to-the-minute news to reinforce our attitudes of opposition to each other and to broadcast propagandist distortions of the truth. Apathy joins despair on the casualty list and then develops into a materialistic state of self-absorption, where all sense of responsibility for others or for the world we share with others is completely lost.

There is no denying the fact that Muslims bear the brunt of many of the aforementioned problems in their particular situations. The prolonged conflict in the Middle East, to name only one example, alerts us to the fact that revolution and reaction and the increasingly sectarian bases to such conflicts are in many places inextricably linked to genuine problems. Social and political inequality, authoritarian and totalitarian forms of government, loss of power of the individual, loss of meaning to life, lack of a decent society are all forms of injustice currently being opposed by Muslims.

If the recent revolutions in these societies - and the tearing apart of a nation's multi-ethnic and multi-religious social fabric is especially tragic - are caused by their social or political conditions, then Muslims living in the liberal democracies of the West are equally oppressed by other kinds of problems specific to where they live. Their limbs may not be at risk from airstrikes or from suicide bombers but their lives and their employment are threatened by economic deprivation and their societies are torn apart by struggles over class, gender and racial distinctions. Sadly, the installation of a Black man in the White House did nothing to limit the serious inequalities to be found in a country that calls itself the champion of civilization. The policy of returning evil with evil is even more widespread. War by means of terrorist activity is now the preferred instrument of regimes in both East and West. Women may enjoy hard-won freedoms but there are many millions who are daily mutilated, sold or widowed in every part of the world. Injustice then is widespread everywhere and a matter of universal concern in the small world we all inhabit today. Bombs and elections disallowed or subverted may seem the special feature of nations outside the West but economic recession, which increases the greed of the few and the suffering of the many, the troubled situation of vulnerable groups such as women, children and the elderly, threats to the environment caused by industrial over-production and over-consumption, those special features of the West and its suppliers, are in truth the collective responsibility of all mankind.

The fact of globalisation can no longer be denied. While its component parts are driven by business motives with the ever-present tendency to ride rough-shod over all, first destroying and then reconstructing always in its own image, globalisation also means that now, more than ever, we inhabit a restricted world. This restriction is most evident in the world of communications with internet and satellite telecommunications and now by the explosion of social media. Our world today is truly connected, an achievement without any historic precedent. As always, we have had to pay a price for this and old traditions and former certainties have been sacrificed en route to the new reality. But the new reality is that humanity is being squeezed into a single global village and this has brought us face to face with further challenges – but with further challenges that may yet be converted into positive outcomes.

The new reality demands that we think globally. This means leaving behind our old parochial interests, looking beyond regional conflicts tied to self-interest, and connecting with all the constituent parts of the global village, to reaffirm our common fellowship in existing connections and to seek out shared aims in new ones. A responsible approach is essential in both cases and success in these new enterprises will depend in very large measure on how we project ourselves and in the ways we communicate with each other.

Thinking in this universal way was once the special talent of the adherents of Islam, its supreme expression being *"And We sent you not except as a mercy unto all the worlds."*[74] Thinking globally was never delimited by notions of spreading God's Word, although when Muslims genuinely did that, they did it rather well.

Traditionally in the spirit of spreading *mercy unto all the worlds*, it meant reaching out, connecting, feeling, caring and sharing. This was when the responsibility was there. Islam never was, and is not, limited to an Arabian identity but was warmly received wherever the message travelled. The appeal of Islam was because of the collective responsibility to care for others and to share, to understand, to respect and to have patience.

Because the world is comprised of diverse elements it therefore is inevitable that differences in cultural outlook or moral standard will persist, yet we must be responsible world-citizens who maintain the truth and correct misconceptions through reason and merciful disposition. Multiculturalism and divergence in belief and persuasion are, in fact, part of God's operation in His universe, "...*Had God so willed, He could surely have made you all one single community; He lets go astray him that wills and guides aright him that wills."*[75] Unity and diversity or, said differently, conformity and divergence, are thus purely a matter of choice. It is in recognition of this freedom of choice that Islam has established diversity and difference of opinion in belief, ideological orientation or lifestyle – evident in the oft-cited verse: *"There shall be no coercion in matters of faith"*[76]

This principle is universal and necessarily transcends all categories of identification. But the freedom to live according to one's own choice is further reinforced by the Qur'an's appeal to authorities, no matter how genuinely benevolent their system or social apparatus, *"And so, exhort them; thy task is only to exhort. Thou canst not compel them to believe."*[77] Coercion is thus denied by Islam, which recognizes the fact that attempts to crush self-government or to silence the voice of conscience may be insidious, and the Qur'an draws attention to the arguments put forward by the Pharaoh, the embodiment of absolutism, *"Said Pharaoh: 'I but want to make you see what I see myself; and I would never make you follow any path but that of rectitude.'"*[78]

Muslims, then, must become responsible world-citizens, fit for purpose in the global village that is the modern world. Of course, there is much that is still positively responsible about Muslims and it is hardly worth mentioning that the overwhelming majority within Islam share humanity's distaste and horror of those who bring religion into disrepute.

The specifically Muslim contribution to the world is evident on many levels and in every walk of life. Beneath the surface representations, Muslims, like any other group within humanity, are peaceable, industrious, creative and, most importantly, humane – and this last aspect is the redeeming quality of all mankind. Muslims are no less adept at invention, both in the past and in the present day, and their input is easily recognizable in the arts and sciences and in commerce and industry. In some instances

Muslim contribution is critical even to the economies of industrially advanced nations. And so, too, in the matter of peaceful coexistence and inter-faith relations. Muslims are a part of the social fabric of many societies in which they are a minority group but their input is substantial.

Seen from the outside, minorities may appear to be less-integrated in societies where Muslims are an identifiable majority with similar perceptions about culturally "unassimilable" Muslims in Western nations. In some cases, perhaps even in many cases, such perceptions are not entirely exaggerated and we have discussed these problems in detail elsewhere. If we speak of responsibility, then our first duty is to confront uncomfortable truths. Real or imagined, intentional or inadvertent, responsibility demands a searching examination of our own guilt. So it was always with the wisest and most responsible ones. Joseph in Egypt, even after being found not guilty, recognized the greater benefits of self-evaluation, *"And yet, I am not trying to absolve myself: for, verily, man's inner self does incite to evil, and saved are only they upon whom my Sustainer bestows His grace. Behold, my Sustainer is much-forgiving, a dispenser of grace!"*[79]

Nevertheless, it must also be conceded that the ordinary man and woman going about the daily business of life in traditionally Muslim societies cannot be blamed for the poor attitudes of vested political interest groups. So there is input on many levels and Muslims cannot be said to be mere spectators, and certainly not fringe-players in the global village.

If Muslims are to take a leading role, that is to say to provide responsible solutions to the many problems in our world, then engagement in the global village must extend beyond modernisation of local economy and infrastructure. Where temporary fixes have failed, they must responsibly apply timeless solutions and promote their special features. Modernisation in predominantly-Muslim countries is impressive in scale, even if rarely pleasing to the eye. In terms of both personnel and expertise, Muslim contribution in the information and banking sectors of the world's economy is significant. World-wide sports audiences regularly marvel at Muslim athletes' combination of skill and effort at the highest level.

Now critics may puzzle at the scale of technological modernisation which hides shortcomings in social and cultural life. The ordinary world citizen may wonder at the value of economic forces that threaten local lives and employment. Although a source of shared pleasure, sporting achievement will not bring social advancement or freedoms.

However, what is still true and still best about Muslim cultural life and Civilization in Islam is the Muslim commitment to caring and sharing, sympathy and empathy. Care of aged parents and care of the very young as well as wealth redistribution through both prescribed and voluntary charity are all still dominant features of Muslim societies. The welfare of an ageing population and debate about how to fund the supposed problem are only now being considered in the nations of the West. Yet Muslims' commitment to their elderly and their young dependents practically defines Islamic societies. Rampant individualism in Western societies all too often leaves the lowest stratum without either opportunity or hope.

The world's wealthiest nations are often keen to export the benefits of political freedom but stumble over social care for the poorest and weakest of their citizens. Of course, there is much to commend and learn from in the welfare models in Western societies, but these social security measures are not immune to economic and political pressures. Muslims, on the other hand, whether economists or businessmen, continue to uphold the enduring value of the *zakat* tithe, which is of course one of the pillars of Islam by which Islam aims at equitable wealth distribution and care for the most vulnerable elements in society, regardless of the political system. Social solidarity may be threatened by irresponsible political interests but Islam's foundational principles of caring and sharing survive and a reaffirmation of these principles is surely the basis of social stability in the long run.

Care of the vulnerable parts of the social body is not, in fact, merely an expedience to ensure stability, stave off unrest or win the popular vote, but an essential prerequisite in Islam. The Qur'an tells us *"Therefore the orphan shalt thou never wrong. And him that seeks thy help shalt thou never chide."*[80] Social welfare as a foundational pillar, built on general participation, receives extensive treatment in the Qur'an but the particular verses just quoted both broaden and deepen the conceptual framework of welfare in Islam. "Orphan", for instance, extends beyond parental loss and connotes one without shelter or protection, both literally and figuratively, while to "never wrong" simultaneously alerts us to a conceptual broadening of "oppression", which takes many forms.

Inequality is the main form of oppression that pervades societies lacking the will to provide for all their constituent parts. Social inequality might raise the spectre of impoverished numbers seeking vengeful retribution against the comfortable minority, but the corrosive effects of inequality ultimately pose a threat to all. In its decadent stagnation, the top layer of society becomes oblivious to the despair and hopelessness of the seething masses. Even without the spectre of revolutions from below, oppression, when it becomes pervasive, has far-reaching consequences.

Disinterest in the socially vulnerable is not only shameful, but takes on the name of oppression, especially when lack of care is juxtaposed with unthinking waste. And "him that seeks thy help never chide" ought also to make us check our stereotyped assumptions about the helpless in society. Can we really ever say that we have done enough or reject others with accusations of laziness? Even in those states where faith in humane society and social care is well-established, the periodical attempts at welfare reform adversely impact on the needy usually in the middle of recession just when the helpless are most vulnerable. For Muslims helping the needy is a central article of faith, a pillar of Islam. Trust in a humanely ordered and justly balanced society regulated through compassion is fundamental to the faith. The fact that compassionate care is an act of worship, joined as a "pillar" of the religion alongside declaration of faith, prayer, fasting and the Hajj commemoration, should awaken in us the sheer importance attached to social provision by the Sustainer. Indeed, God makes explicit the relationship of Faith, Prayer and Charity. *"True piety does not consist in turning your faces towards East or West, but truly pious are they who believe in God, and the Last Day, and the angels, and Revelation, and the prophets, and spend their substance – however much they themselves may cherish it – upon their near kin, and the orphans, and the needy, and the wayfarer, and the beggars, and for the freeing of human beings from bondage, and are constant in prayer, and render the purifying dues..."*[81]

We might note that the *zakat* tithe that guarantees charity is described as a "purifying due". There already exists an extensive body of scholarly interpretation concerning the "purification of wealth" but our particular focus here is the link with faith and accountability. God says, *"Hence, accept that part of their possessions which is offered for the sake of God so that thou mayest cleanse them and cause them to grow in purity..."*[82] As "purification" is conceptually related to the absolution of sin or the "oppression of the self", so charity represents a practical act of atonement. We might also add by the way that the Qur'an chapter that contains the verse is appropriately named *"Repentance"*. Furthermore, in Islam, too, charity logically begins at home but, as an expression of humanity, Islam's welfare model recognizes no social boundaries, *"Hence, give his due to the near of kin, as well as the needy and the wayfarer; that is best for all who seek God's countenance: it is they, they that shall attain to a happy state."*[83]

From a Muslim perspective, then, the broad basis of responsibility is already there. Why not now promote the in-built special features of

93

Muslim cultural life throughout the global village? Neither revolt and reaction nor lip-service to Revelation will solve humanity's questions. The real contribution is a collective responsibility and a projection of mercy unto "all the worlds".

The problems that beset humanity stem from injustice, the very opposite of mercy and compassion. Fair dealing underscores our notions of what is humane and compassionate interaction is what separates us from the animal world. Never confined to legal systems and judicial processes, humanity is meant to take on this major attribute of God so that justice becomes simultaneously God-consciousness and the respecting of His Attribute. God Himself expresses it in this way, *"Myself, I have proscribed injustice, and oppression is proscribed among you, so do not be unjust to one another."*[84] Through this mankind is commanded *"...Bear witness to the truth in all equity, and never let hatred of anyone lead you into the sin of deviating from justice; be just, – this is closest to God-consciousness..."*[85]

It is because justice is an automatic consequence of all that is humane, that human dignity insists on freedom from oppression. Whereas human rights may be relative, as for instance when they may have to be denied or forfeited as in the case of a convicted criminal in a civil society, human dignity, on the other hand, is inalienable as endowed by the Creator, *"We have, indeed, conferred dignity on the children of Adam [...] and favoured them far above most of Our Creation."*[86] In truth responsible conduct, whether charity or fair-dealing, is nothing other than God-consciousness, so that it is responsibility synonymous with humane conduct that raises mankind to high dignity, *"O mankind! Behold, We have created you all out of a male and a female, and have made you into nations and tribes, so that you might come to know one another. Verily, the noblest of you in the Sight of God is the one who is most deeply conscious of Him."*[87]

Where and when human dignity is assured the rights of the human being inevitably follow. It is for this reason that mankind was appointed vicegerent – with all the responsibilities that go with the stewardship of our known universe. It is Islam's special function to raise awareness of Man's high dignity, common biological origin and the primacy of inter-relations *"that you might come to know one another"*. And, if we seriously take Revelation as guidance, we are to constantly remember our responsibilities.

References

1. Bukhari, Sahih: 2004
2. Tirmidhi, Sahih: 3984
3. Bukhari: 1312
4. Bukhari: 1356
5. Bukhari: 2916
6. Qur'an, Al Ahzab, 33:21
7. Sometimes referred to as the "Constitution of Madinah". The present author, however, cannot agree with the designation "constitution", which has technical associations appropriate to the framework of a state, and has preferred the term "charter", which defines rights and liberties, to describe the instrument of the Madinah Declaration. Early Muslim sources that refer to the Declaration include the historian Muhammad Ibn Ishaq in his Sirat. Scholars subsequently have attempted to define it as a "constitution" or "treaty". The Declaration perhaps accords to the idea of a social contract or charter.
8. Q, Al Baqarah, 2:256
9. Q, Al Kahf, 18:29
10. Q, Al Maeda, 5:48
11. Q, Al Kaafiroon, 109:6
12. Al Kaafiroon, 109:1
13. Al Baqarah, 2:44
14. Q, Ankabut, 29:46
15. Q, Al Israa, 17:70
16. Qadi Abu Ishaq Ismail ibn Ishaq, b. 200AH–d. 282AH
17. Q, Al Mumtahinha, 60:8
18. Ahmad, Musnad: 2018
19. Bukhari: 69
20. Al 'Israa, 17:70
21. Q, Al Hujurat, 49:13
22. Ahmad, Musnad: 22391
23. Q, Al Mulk, 67:14
24. Q, An Nahl, 16:93
25. Ibn Shaybah, Musannaf: 54
26. Al Hujurat, 49:13
27. Ibn Hibban, Sahih: 1704
28. Bukhari: 30
29. See, for example, Islam and the World: the Rise and Decline of Muslims by A.H.A. Nadwi

30. Ibn Katheer, Tafsir: 1/388
31. Abu Dawud, Sunan: 5121
32. Bukhari: 4907
33. Al Kahf, 18:51
34. Q, Ar Rum, 30:9
35. Q, At Tawbah, 9:72
36. Q, Al Alaq, 96:1-5
37. Al Haithami; Al Mujma al-Zawa'id: 2/19; and Ibn Katheer; Al Bidaya wa an-Nihaya: 3/214
38. Bukhari: 1/168
39. Al Israa, 17:70
40. Al Mulk, 67:15
41. Al Baqarah, 2:34
42. Q, Muhammad, 47:119
43. Q, Al Mujadalah, 58:11
44. Al Baqarah, 2:31
45. Ibn Majah, Sunan: 1/81
46. Tabarani, Tafsir (S. Al Hijr)
47. Al Israa, 17:44
48. Bukhari: 3/1205
49. Bukhari: 2/833
50. Tirmidhi, 1378; and Abu Dawud; 3083
51. Al Mulk, 67:14
52. Q, Al Fatiha, 1:6
53. Q, Al Hashr, 59:19
54. Al Baqarah, 2:136
55. Al Baqarah, 2:83
56. Muslim, Sahih: 2365
57. Bukhari, Al Adab Al Mufrad: 273
58. Al Baqarah, 2:183
59. Q, Maryam, 19:31-32 59.
60. Al Ahzab, 33:7-8
61. Q, Al Ambiyaa, 21:107
62. Al Israa, 17:106
63. Al Baqarah, 2:151
64. Al Ahzab, 33:21
65. Q, Al Qalam, 68:4
66. Bukhari, Al Adab Al Mufrad: 234
67. Q, Aal 'Imran, 3:31

68. Bukhari: 5785
69. Ahmad: 16/99
70. Muslim: 772
71. Muslim; 4678
72. Al Hujurat, 49:6
73. Q, Al Anfal, 8:38
74. Al Ambiya, 21:107
75.An Nahl, 16:93
76. Al Baqarah, 2:256
77.Q, Al Ghashiya, 88:21-22
78.Q, Ghafir, 40:29
79. Q, Yusuf, 12:53
80. Q, Ad Duha, 93:9-10
81.Al Baqarah, 2:177
82.At Tawba, 9:103
83. Ar Rum, 30:38
84. Muslim, Ch. Prohibition of Oppression
85. Al Maeda, 5:8
86. Al Israa, 17:70
87. Al Hujurat, 49:13

Bibliography

Abu Dawud, Sulaiman, *Sunan Abu Dawud*

Ad-Dhahabi, *Siyaar A'lam an-Nubaala*

Al Abbas, ibn Abd-al-Muttalib, *The Illumination of Heaven and Earth* in *Ash-Shifah*, Qadi 'Iyad ibn Musa al-Yahsubi

Al-Baihaqi, Ahmad ibn Hussain, *Shuab Al-Eman*

Al Haithami, Ali ibn Abu Bakr, *Al Mujma al-Zawa'id wa Manba al-Fawa'id*

An-Nawawi, Muhiuddin Yahya ibn Sharaf, *Al Arba'in*

Asad, Muhammad, trans. and commentary, *The Message of the Qur'an*, The Book Foundation, Bristol, 2003

As-Suyuti, Jalal ad-Din, *Tarikh Al-Khullafa*   At-Tabari, Muhammad ibn Jarir, *Tafsir (Surat Al Hijr)*

At-Tabarani, Sulaiman ibn Ahmad, *Tabarani Al-Awsat*

At-Tirmidhi, Abu Isa Muhammad, *Jame at-Tirmidhi* Bukhari, Muhammad ibn Ismail, *Al-Jame as-Sahih – Adab al-Mufrad*

Ibn Abbas, Abdullah, *Tafsir ibn Abbas*

Ibn Abi Shaybah, Abd-Allah ibn Muhammad, *Musannaf*

Ibn Hanbal, Ahmad ibn Muhammad, *Musnad Ahmad*

Ibn Hibban, Abu Hatim Muhammad, *Al-Jame as-Sahih*

Ibn 'Iyad al-Yahsubi, Abul Fadl 'Iyad ibn Musa, *Muhammad, Messenger of Allah*, or *Ash-Shifah*

Ibn Katheer, Ismail; *Al Bidaya wa an-Nihaya*, or *Tarikh ibn Katheer* Ibn Majah, Muhammad ibn Yazid, *Sunan Ibn Majah*

Ibn Zuhair, Kaab, *Banat Su'ad*

Muslim, ibn Hajjaj, *Al-Jame as-Sahih*

Nadwi, Abul Hassan Ali, *Islam and the World: the Rise and Decline of Muslims*, UK Islamic Academy, 2005